Selected Poems

Crofts Classics

GENERAL EDITOR

Samuel H. Beer, *Harvard University*

WILLIAM WORDSWORTH

Selected
Poems

EDITED BY

George W. Meyer

Harlan Davidson, Inc.
Wheeling, Illinois 60090-6000

Copyright © 1950
Harlan Davidson, Inc.

Library of Congress Cataloging-in-Publication Data

Wordsworth, William, 1770–1850.
  Selected poems.

  (Crofts classics)
  Bibliography: p. 115
  1. Meyer, George W. (George Wilbur) II. Title.
PR5853.M49   1985   821'.7   85–25766
ISBN 0-88295-103-3 (pbk.)

Manufactured in the United States of America
01 00 99 98 23 MG

CONTENTS

INTRODUCTION

WILLIAM Wordsworth is read and admired by a great many readers for a great variety of reasons. Ornithologists are grateful for his tributes to the cuckoo, the green linnet, and the skylark, and for his inspiration of William Cullen Bryant to the further poetic celebration of birds. Horticulturists enjoy Wordsworth's sympathetic understanding of the daisy and the primrose, and the knowledge that the great man was no mean landscape gardener himself. Lexicographers delight in his vocabulary, and find his poetry more useful than that of any other recent writer for purposes of quotation in Modern English dictionaries. Literary historians honor Wordsworth for having simultaneously locked the door on Neo-Classicism and thrown wide the portals of English verse to the Romantic Movement. Makers of moral manuals for the young discover in his collected works specifications for the "Ideal Man" and the "Ideal Woman." And those who like to psychoanalyze the poets of their choice find ample food for speculation in Wordsworth's biography.

But the appeal Wordsworth makes to readers with interests so personal and specialized as these hardly explains why it is that within a century of his death Wordsworth has come to be regarded by lovers of poetry for its own sake as one of the greatest of English poets. To understand this, and to understand why he should be read by everyone with a claim to literacy in English, we must discover the more general and less esoteric qualities of his thought and verse. And in order to do this, we must first know how to approach him.

Anyone who reads Wordsworth in a casual, half-hearted fashion is susceptible to ideas that may prove embarrassing in well-informed circles. Such a reader might suppose that Wordsworth was a queer sort of man who fell into articulate delirium at the sight of daffodils, loved idiot boys, and spent his time interviewing decrepit old people like the persevering leech-gatherer in *Resolution and Independence.* Or he might imagine that Wordsworth detested formal education, wrote down whatever came into his head "spontaneously," and greatly preferred sitting on old gray stones to the reading of books. No careful reader will form such opinions, and Wordsworth must be read carefully. To get the most out of him, or any other writer of complexity, we must become active, co-operative readers. As he himself insisted in his Essay, Supplementary to the Preface of 1815, the reader cannot expect to be carried by the poet "like an Indian prince or general—stretched on his palanquin, and borne by slaves." The reader must work. He must exert himself and bring to the reading of a poem a portion of the intense concentration and sustained energy which the poet himself expended on its composition. Wordsworth spent two years writing the *Intimations Ode;* the reader has not been born who can understand it overnight.

Wordsworth should be closely read by everyone simply because he tells us more that is important about human nature and the world we inhabit than any English writer since Shakespeare. It is a commonplace, exploited by many parodists who enjoy making fun of their betters, that Wordsworth not only wrote but published more bad verse than any other major writer. That is not what matters. Wordsworth is the greatest philosophical poet to write in the English language. His best reflective lyrics, *Tintern Abbey* and the *Intimations Ode,* are notable for their profundity of thought and majesty of tone. His sonnets are unequalled in variety of subject, eloquence of expression, and nobility of sentiment. Many of them, written when England lay under a threat of foreign invasion no less grave than the one offered by Hitler's Nazis in 1940-41, ever since have been an unfailing source of English strength in time of desperate national need. In addition to these accomplishments, Wordsworth revolutionized the language of English poetry, wrote the Prefaces to *Lyrical Ballads*—among the greatest of all contributions to literary theory and criticism—and, in *The Prelude,* his long autobiographical poem, left us a full length account of the development of a major poetic imagination, from which we gain deep insight into the psychology of the poet and the mysteries of the act of literary creation.

One of the basic tenets of Wordsworth's philosophy is that the world and everything in it, man included, are good, and that it is mankind's fundamental duty to enjoy "the air it breathes." The poet's prime responsibility is to assist mankind towards the enthusiastic acceptance of the dynamic life in nature made possible for all of us by a benef-icent God who is both immanent and transcendant. According to Wordsworth, the poet himself is an essentially happy person who works under one restriction only, that of giving pleasure to his readers. It is important to understand what Wordsworth meant by "pleasure." He did not mean the kind of excitement from danger experienced vicariously by the reader of Gothic tales of horror, the eighteenth-century equivalents of present-day detective stories. Nor did he have in mind the static and sterile intellectual gratification gained by the reader who solves the double-crostics that make up too large a part of twentieth-century poetry. The pleasure Wordsworth thought the poet should provide was the sense of well-being left in the reader after his entire personality, intellectual and emotional, had participated actively in a microcosmic literary experience. Hence it was that to Wordsworth poetry was a comprehensive affirmation, "an acknowledgement of the beauty of the universe" and the "image of man and nature." And hence it was that Wordsworth could find poetry every-where: in the song of a bird, in the sight of the sleeping city of London, in the imagined death of a girl with whom he imagined himself in love, in the triumphant defeat of Toussaint L'Ouverture, in the magical mutations produced by memory on past experience, or in the inconsolable grief of a little girl who had lost her ragged coat.

The publication of his first poems, *An Evening Walk* and *Descriptive Sketches,* coincided with the declaration of war between France and England in 1793; and the first collected edition of his poems appeared in 1815, the year which saw the overthrow of Napoleon at Waterloo and the end of Wordsworth's great creative period. Were it not for the political sonnets and an occasional passage in *The Prelude* or *The Excursion* we would hardly guess that Wordsworth's best poetry was written when England was struggling for life in the first of the three terrible ordeals she has successfully withstood within the last century and a half. This is not because Wordsworth was shut up in an ivory tower, indifferent to the fate of his country and his fellow men. When the danger was greatest, Wordsworth, despite the exemption his family responsibilities gave him, donned a red coat with the Ambleside volunteers and prepared to repel the impending assault. Those who wish further concrete evidence of the poet's immense and expert knowledge of international affairs and military strategy may consult his prose tract on the Convention of Cintra and his extraordinary letter of 28 March 1811 to Captain Pasley of the Royal Engineers.

Wordsworth neglected the war and Napoleon in his major poems because he knew that wars and Napoleons are eccentric and transitory, and therefore not of lasting importance. To be happy, man must become familiar with and adjust to the immutable laws of nature. These include the laws of the mind of man—"My haunt, and the main region of my song," as Wordsworth put it in *The Recluse*. Only when this has been accomplished will human society be governed by the harmony and joy characteristic of "Nature's holy plan," and only then will that "image of a better time," the pattern of a perfect life prefigured in *The Prelude* at last have been achieved. The way to this happy goal lies through the simple and the ordinary, the enduring and the permanent. Wordsworth knew the road. That is why those who know him best claim for his poetry what the Wanderer in *The Excursion* (IV, 1142-1147) claimed for the universe of nature:

> . . . there are times,
> I doubt not, when to you it doth impart
> Authentic tidings of invisible things;
> Of ebb and flow, and ever-during power;
> And central peace, subsisting at the heart
> Of endless agitation.

PRINCIPAL DATES IN THE LIFE OF WILLIAM WORDSWORTH

❧

1770 (April 7) William Wordsworth born at Cocker-mouth in Cumberland. Dorothy Wordsworth born the following year (1771).

1787 Enters St. John's College, Cambridge.

1789 *Outbreak of the French Revolution.*

1790 Wordsworth and Robert Jones go on a walking tour through France and Switzerland in the long vacation.

1791 Wordsworth graduates B. A., Cambridge, and goes to France.

1792 Residence at Orleans and Blois; friendship with Michel Beaupuy; birth of Caroline, daughter of Wordsworth and Annette Vallon. Returns to England.

1793 Publishes *An Evening Walk* and *Descriptive Sketches. Outbreak of war between England and France; the Reign of Terror in France.* Wordsworth writes his *Letter to the Bishop of Llandaff* and begins *Guilt and Sorrow.*

1794 Acts as nurse to Raisley Calvert, from whom he inherits £900.

1795 Settles with Dorothy at Racedown; meets Samuel Taylor Coleridge at Bristol.

1797 The Wordsworths move to Alfoxden to be near Coleridge at Nether Stowey.

1798 Wordsworth projects *The Recluse* and begins *The Prelude. Lyrical Ballads* published. Coleridge and the Wordsworths spend the winter and spring of 1798-1799 in Germany.

1799 Wordsworth and Dorothy settle at Dove Cottage, Grasmere, Westmorland.

1800   Second edition of *Lyrical Ballads* published, with Preface.

1802   *Peace of Amiens.* Wordsworth pays a brief visit to France, then, on his return, marries Mary Hutchinson (October 4).

1803   *War between England and France resumed.*

1804   *Ode to Duty* written; *Intimations Ode* (begun 1802) completed. Composition of *The Prelude* resumed.

1805   John Wordsworth drowned (February 5). *The Prelude* completed.

1807   *Poems in Two Volumes* published.

1808-1814   The Wordsworths move to Allan Bank (1808), thence to The Rectory (1811), and finally to Rydal Mount (1813). Wordsworth writes the prose tract on *The Convention of Cintra* (published 1809), becomes Distributor of Stamps for Westmorland (1813), and publishes *The Excursion* (1814).

1815   *Battle of Waterloo and final defeat of Napoleon.* First collected edition of Wordsworth's poems published.

1818   Wordsworth active in Westmorland politics.

1820   *Death of George III.* Wordsworth publishes *The River Duddon: a Series of Sonnets.*

1822   *Ecclesiastical Sketches* published.

1837   *Accession of Queen Victoria.*

1843   Wordsworth becomes Poet Laureate.

1850   (23 April) Death of Wordsworth. *The Prelude* published posthumously.

SELECTED POEMS OF
WILLIAM WORDSWORTH

Preface to Lyrical Ballads

THE FIRST Volume of these Poems has already been sub-
mitted to general perusal. It was published as an experi-
ment, which I hoped might be of some use to ascertain how
far, by fitting to metrical arrangement a selection of the
real language of men in a state of vivid sensation, that
sort of pleasure and that quantity of pleasure may be im-
parted, which a Poet may rationally endeavor to impart.

I had formed no very inaccurate estimate of the probable
effect of those Poems: I flattered myself that they who
should be pleased with them would read them with more
than common pleasure: and, on the other hand, I was well
aware that by those who should dislike them they would
be read with more than common dislike. The result has
differed from my expectation in this only, that a greater
number have been pleased than I ventured to hope I should
please.

Several of my Friends are anxious for the success of these
Poems, from a belief that, if the views with which they
were composed were indeed realized, a class of Poetry
would be produced, well adapted to interest mankind per-
manently, and not unimportant in the quality and in the
multiplicity of its moral relations: and on this account they
have advised me to prefix a systematic defence of the theory
upon which the Poems were written. But I was unwilling
to undertake the task, knowing that on this occasion the
Reader would look coldly upon my arguments, since I
might be suspected of having been principally influenced
by the selfish and foolish hope of *reasoning* him into an
approbation of these particular Poems; and I was still more
unwilling to undertake the task, because adequately to dis-

play the opinions, and fully to enforce the arguments, would require a space wholly disproportionate to a preface. For to treat the subject with the clearness and coherence of which it is susceptible, it would be necessary to give a full account of the present state of the public taste in this country, and to determine how far this taste is healthy or depraved; which, again, could not be determined, without pointing out in what manner language and the human mind act and re-act on each other, and without retracing the revolutions, not of literature alone, but likewise of society itself. I have therefore altogether declined to enter regularly upon this defence; yet I am sensible that there would be something like impropriety in abruptly obtruding upon the Public, without a few words of introduction, Poems so materially different from those upon which general approbation is at present bestowed.

It is supposed that by the act of writing in verse an Author makes a formal engagement that he will gratify certain known habits of association; that he not only thus apprises the Reader that certain classes of ideas and expressions will be found in his book, but that others will be carefully excluded. This exponent or symbol held forth by metrical language must in different eras of literature have excited very different expectations: for example, in the age of Catullus, Terence, and Lucretius,[1] and that of Statius or Claudian;[2] and in our own country, in the age of Shakespeare and Beaumont and Fletcher, and that of Donne and Cowley, or Dryden, or Pope. I will not take upon me to determine the exact import of the promise which, by the act of writing in verse, an Author in the present day makes to his reader; but it will undoubtedly appear to many persons that I have not fulfilled the terms of an engagement thus voluntarily contracted. They who have been accustomed to the gaudiness and inane phrase-

[1] **Catullus** (87-54 B.C.) was a Roman lyric poet whom Wordsworth imitated in his youth. **Terence** (190-159 B.C.) wrote Latin comedies. **Lucretius** (95-55 B.C.) was the author of *De rerum natura,* a famous philosophical poem. Wordsworth admired these writers for their naturalness of style.

[2] **Statius** (61-96) was a Latin epic poet the first book of whose *Thebaid* was translated by Pope. **Claudian** (365-408) was a late Roman poet whose style Wordsworth regarded as artificial.

ology of many modern writers, if they persist in reading this book to its conclusion, will, no doubt, frequently have to struggle with feelings of strangeness and awkwardness: they will look round for poetry, and will be induced to inquire by what species of courtesy these attempts can be permitted to assume that title. I hope, therefore, the reader will not censure me for attempting to state what I have proposed to myself to perform; and also (as far as the limits of a preface will permit) to explain some of the chief reasons which have determined me in the choice of my purpose: that at least he may be spared any unpleasant feeling of disappointment, and that I myself may be protected from one of the most dishonorable accusations which can be brought against an Author; namely, that of an indolence which prevents him from endeavoring to ascertain what is his duty, or, when his duty is ascertained, prevents him from performing it.

The principal object, then, proposed in these Poems was to choose incidents and situations from common life, and to relate or describe them, throughout, as far as was possible in a selection of language really used by men, and, at the same time, to throw over them a certain coloring of imagination, whereby ordinary things should be presented to the mind in an unusual aspect; and further, and above all, to make these incidents and situations interesting by tracing in them, truly though not ostentatiously, the primary laws of our nature: chiefly, as far as regards the manner in which we associate ideas in a state of excitement. Humble and rustic life was generally chosen, because in that condition the essential passions of the heart find a better soil in which they can attain their maturity, are less under restraint, and speak a plainer and more emphatic language; because in that condition of life our elementary feelings coëxist in a state of greater simplicity, and consequently may be more accurately contemplated and more forcibly communicated; because the manners of rural life germinate from those elementary feelings, and, from the necessary character of rural occupations, are more easily comprehended, and are more durable; and, lastly, because in that condition the passions of men are incorporated with the beautiful and permanent forms of nature. The language, too, of these men has been adopted (purified indeed from what appear to be its real defects, from all lasting and rational causes of dislike or disgust) because such men hourly communicate with the best objects from which the best part of language is originally derived; and because, from their rank in society and the sameness and narrow circle of their intercourse, being less under the influence of social vanity, they convey their feelings and notions in simple and unelaborated expressions. Accordingly, such a language, arising out of repeated experience and regular feelings, is a more permanent and a far more philosophical language than that which is frequently substituted for it by Poets, who think that they are conferring honor upon themselves and their art, in proportion as they separate themselves from the sympathies of men, and indulge in arbitrary and capricious habits of expression, in order to furnish food for fickle tastes, and fickle appetites, of their own creation.

I cannot, however, be insensible to the present outcry against the triviality and meanness, both of thought and language, which some of my contemporaries have occasion-ally introduced into their metrical compositions; and I acknowledge that this defect, where it exists, is more dis-honorable to the Writer's own character than false refine-ment or arbitrary innovation, though I should contend at the same time that it is far less pernicious in the sum of its consequences. From such verses the poems in these volumes will be found distinguished at least by one mark of differ-ence, that each of them has a worthy *purpose*. Not that I always began to write with a distinct purpose formally conceived; but habits of meditation have, I trust, so prompted and regulated my feelings, that my descriptions of such objects as strongly excite those feelings will be found to carry along with them a *purpose*. If this opinion be erroneous, I can have little right to the name of a Poet. For all good poetry is the spontaneous overflow of powerful feelings: and though this be true, Poems to which any value can be attached were never produced on any variety of subjects but by a man who, being possessed of more than usual organic sensibility, had also thought long and deeply. For our continued influxes of feeling are modified and directed by our thoughts, which are indeed the repre-sentatives of all our past feelings; and, as by contemplating the relation of these general representatives to each other, we discover what is really important to men, so, by the repetition and continuance of this act, our feelings will be connected with important subjects, till at length, if we be originally possessed of much sensibility, such habits of mind will be produced that, by obeying blindly and mechanically the impulses of those habits, we shall describe objects, and utter sentiments, of such a nature, and in such connection with each other, that the understanding of the Reader must necessarily be in some degree enlightened, and his affections strengthened and purified.

It has been said that each of these Poems has a purpose. Another circumstance must be mentioned which distinguishes these Poems from the popular Poetry of the day; it is this, that the feeling therein developed gives importance to the action and situation, and not the action and situation to the feeling.

A sense of false modesty shall not prevent me from asserting that the Reader's attention is pointed to this mark of distinction, far less for the sake of these particular Poems than from the general importance of the subject. The subject is indeed important! For the human mind is capable of being excited without the application of gross and violent stimulants; and he must have a very faint perception of its beauty and dignity who does not know this, and who does not further know that one being is elevated above another in proportion as he possesses this capability. It has therefore appeared to me that to endeavor to produce or enlarge this capability is one of the best services in which, at any period, a Writer can be engaged; but this service, excellent at all times, is especially so at the present day. For a multitude of causes, unknown to former times, are now acting with a combined force to blunt the discriminating powers of the mind, and, unfitting it for all voluntary exertion, to reduce it to a state of almost savage torpor. The most effective of these causes are the great national events which are daily taking place, and the increasing accumulation of men in cities, where the uniformity of their occupations produces a craving for extraordinary incident, which the rapid communication of intelligence hourly gratifies. To this tendency of life and manners the literature and theatrical exhibitions of the country have

conformed themselves. The invaluable works of our elder
writers, I had almost said the works of Shakespeare and
Milton, are driven into neglect by frantic novels, sickly and
stupid German Tragedies, and deluges of idle and extrava-
gant stories in verse.[1] When I think upon this degrading
thirst after outrageous stimulation, I am almost ashamed
to have spoken of the feeble endeavor made in these
volumes to counteract it; and, reflecting upon the magni-
tude of the general evil, I should be oppressed with no
dishonorable melancholy, had I not a deep impression of
certain inherent and indestructible qualities of the human
mind, and likewise of certain powers in the great and per-
manent objects that act upon it, which are equally inherent
and indestructible; and were there not added to this im-
pression a belief that the time is approaching when the evil
will be systematically opposed, by men of greater powers,
and with far more distinguished success.

Having dwelt thus long on the subjects and aim of these
Poems, I shall request the Reader's permission to apprise
him of a few circumstances relating to their *style*, in order,
among other reasons, that he may not censure me for not
having performed what I never attempted. The Reader will
find that personifications of abstract ideas rarely occur in
these volumes, and are utterly rejected, as an ordinary de-
vice to elevate the style, and raise it above prose. My pur-
pose was to imitate, and, as far as possible, to adopt the
very language of men; and assuredly such personifications
do not make any natural or regular part of that language.
They are, indeed, a figure of speech occasionally prompted
by passion, and I have made use of them as such; but have
endeavored utterly to reject them as a mechanical device of
style, or as a family language which Writers in metre seem
to lay claim to by prescription. I have wished to keep the
Reader in the company of flesh and blood, persuaded that
by so doing I shall interest him. Others who pursue a
different track will interest him likewise; I do not interfere

[1] In this and the two preceding sentences Wordsworth refers to
the war between France and England, the population shifts
caused by the Industrial and Agrarian Revolutions, the "Gothic"
novels of such writers as Ann Radcliffe and "Monk" Lewis, and
translations of the melodramas of the German playwright, August
von Kotzebue.

with their claim, but wish to prefer a claim of my own. There will also be found in these volumes little of what is usually called poetic diction; as much pains has been taken to avoid it as is ordinarily taken to produce it; this has been done for the reason already alleged, to bring my language near to the language of men; and further, because the pleasure which I have proposed to myself to impart is of a kind very different from that which is supposed by many persons to be the proper object of poetry. Without being culpably particular, I do not know how to give my Reader a more exact notion of the style in which it was my wish and intention to write, than by informing him that I have at all times endeavored to look steadily at my subject; consequently there is, I hope, in these Poems little falsehood of description, and my ideas are expressed in language fitted to their respective importance. Something must have been gained by this practice, as it is friendly to one property of all good poetry, namely, good sense: but it has necessarily cut me off from a large portion of phrases and figures of speech which from father to son have long been regarded as the common inheritance of Poets. I have also thought it expedient to restrict myself still further, having abstained from the use of many expressions, in themselves proper and beautiful, but which have been foolishly repeated by bad Poets, till such feelings of disgust are connected with them as it is scarcely possible by any art of association to overpower.

If in a poem there should be found a series of lines, or even a single line, in which the language, though naturally arranged, and according to the strict laws of metre, does not differ from that of prose, there is a numerous class of critics, who, when they stumble upon these prosaisms, as they call them, imagine that they have made a notable discovery, and exult over the Poet as over a man ignorant of his own profession. Now these men would establish a canon of criticism which the Reader will conclude he must utterly reject, if he wishes to be pleased with these volumes. And it would be a most easy task to prove to him that not only the language of a large portion of every good poem, even of the most elevated character, must necessarily, except with reference to the metre, in no respect differ from that of good prose, but likewise that some of the most interesting

parts of the best poems will be found to be strictly the
language of prose when prose is well written. The truth of
this assertion might be demonstrated by innumerable pas-
sages from almost all the poetical writings, even of Milton
himself. To illustrate the subject in a general manner, I
will here adduce a short composition of Gray, who was at
the head of those who, by their reasonings, have attempted
to widen the space of separation betwixt Prose and Metrical
composition, and was more than any other man curiously
elaborate in the structure of his own poetic diction.

> In vain to me the smiling mornings shine,
> And reddening Phoebus lifts his golden fire:
> The birds in vain their amorous descant join,
> Or cheerful fields resume their green attire.
> These ears, alas! for other notes repine;
> *A different object do these eyes require;*
> *My lonely anguish melts no heart but mine;*
> *And in my breast the imperfect joys expire;*
> Yet morning smiles the busy race to cheer,
> And new-born pleasure brings to happier men;
> The fields to all their wonted tribute bear;
> To warm their little loves the birds complain.
> *I fruitless mourn to him that cannot hear,*
> *And weep the more because I weep in vain.*

It will easily be perceived, that the only part of this
Sonnet which is of any value is the lines printed in Italics;
it is equally obvious that, except in the rhyme, and in the
use of the single word "fruitless" for fruitlessly, which is
so far a defect, the language of these lines does in no
respect differ from that of prose.

By the foregoing quotation it has been shown that the
language of Prose may yet be well adapted to Poetry; and
it was previously asserted that a large portion of the lan-
guage of every good poem can in no respect differ from
that of good Prose. We will go further. It may be safely
affirmed that there neither is, nor can be, any *essential* dif-
ference between the language of prose and metrical com-
position. We are fond of tracing the resemblance be-
tween Poetry and Painting, and, accordingly, we call
them Sisters: but where shall we find bonds of connection
sufficiently strict to typify the affinity betwixt metrical

and prose composition? They both speak by and to the same organs; the bodies in which both of them are clothed may be said to be of the same substance, their affections are kindred, and almost identical, not necessarily differing even in degree; Poetry sheds no tears "such as Angels weep," but natural and human tears; she can boast of no celestial ichor that distinguishes her vital juices from those of Prose; the same human blood circulates through the veins of them both.

If it be affirmed that rhyme and metrical arrangement of themselves constitute a distinction which overturns what has just been said on the strict affinity of metrical language with that of Prose, and paves the way for other artificial distinctions which the mind voluntarily admits,[1] I answer that the language of such Poetry as is here recommended is, as far as is possible, a selection of the language really spoken by men; that this selection, wherever it is made with true taste and feeling, will of itself form a distinction far greater than would at first be imagined, and will entirely separate the composition from the vulgarity and meanness of ordinary life; and, if metre be superadded thereto, I believe that a dissimilitude will be produced altogether sufficient for the gratification of a rational mind. What other distinction would we have? Whence is it to come? And where is it to exist? Not, surely, where the Poet speaks through the mouths of his characters: it cannot be necessary here, either for elevation of style, or any of its supposed ornaments: for, if the Poet's subject be judiciously chosen, it will naturally, and upon fit occasion, lead him to passions the language of which, if selected truly and judiciously, must necessarily be dignified and variegated, and alive with metaphors and figures. I forbear to speak of an incongruity which would shock the intelligent Reader, should the Poet interweave any foreign splendor of his own with that which the passion naturally suggests: it is sufficient to say that such addition is unnecessary. And surely it is more probable that those passages which with propriety abound with metaphors and figures will have their due effect, if, upon other occasions where the passions are of a

[1] Here begins the important passage added to the Preface by Wordsworth in the edition of 1802.

milder character, the style also be subdued and temperate.

But as the pleasure which I hope to give by the Poems now presented to the Reader must depend entirely on just notions upon this subject, and as it is in itself of high importance to our taste and moral feelings, I cannot content myself with these detached remarks. And if, in what I am about to say, it shall appear to some that my labor is unnecessary, and that I am like a man fighting a battle without enemies, such persons may be reminded that, whatever be the language outwardly holden by men, a practical faith in the opinions which I am wishing to establish is almost unknown. If my conclusions are admitted, and carried as far as they must be carried if admitted at all, our judgments concerning the works of the greatest Poets both ancient and modern will be far different from what they are at present, both when we praise, and when we censure; and our moral feelings influencing and influenced by these judgments will, I believe, be corrected and purified.

Taking up the subject, then, upon general grounds, let me ask, what is meant by the word Poet? What is a Poet? To whom does he address himself? And what language is to be expected from him?—He is a man speaking to men: a man, it is true, endowed with more lively sensibility, more enthusiasm and tenderness, who has a greater knowledge of human nature, and a more comprehensive soul, than are supposed to be common among mankind; a man pleased with his own passions and volitions, and who rejoices more than other men in the spirit of life that is in him; delighting to contemplate similar volitions and passions as manifested in the goings-on of the Universe, and habitually impelled to create them where he does not find them. To these qualities he has added a disposition to be affected more than other men by absent things as if they were present; an ability of conjuring up in himself passions which are indeed far from being the same as those produced by real events, yet (especially in those parts of the general sympathy which are pleasing and delightful) do more nearly resemble the passions produced by real events than anything which, from the motions of their own minds merely, other men are accustomed to feel in themselves:—whence, and from practice, he has acquired a greater readiness and power in expressing what he thinks and feels, and especially those thoughts and feelings which, by his own choice, or from the structure of his own mind, arise in him without immediate external excitement.

But whatever portion of this faculty we may suppose even the greatest Poet to possess, there cannot be a doubt that the language which it will suggest to him must often, in liveliness and truth, fall short of that which is uttered by men in real life under the actual pressure of those passions, certain shadows of which the Poet thus produces, or feels to be produced, in himself.

However exalted a notion we would wish to cherish of the character of a Poet, it is obvious that while he describes and imitates passions, his employment is in some degree mechanical, compared with the freedom and power of real and substantial action and suffering. So that it will be the wish of the Poet to bring his feelings near to those of the persons whose feelings he describes,—nay, for short spaces of time, perhaps, to let himself slip into an entire delusion, and even confound and identify his own feelings with theirs; modifying only the language which is thus suggested to him by a consideration that he describes for a particular purpose, that of giving pleasure. Here, then, he will apply the principle of selection which has been already insisted upon. He will depend upon this for removing what would otherwise be painful or disgusting in the passion; he will feel that there is no necessity to trick out or to elevate nature: and, the more industriously he applies this principle, the deeper will be his faith that no words which *his* fancy or imagination can suggest will be to be compared with those which are the emanations of reality and truth.

But it may be said by those who do not object to the general spirit of these remarks, that, as it is impossible for the Poet to produce upon all occasions language as exquisitely fitted for the passion as that which the real passion itself suggests, it is proper that he should consider himself as in the situation of a translator, who does not scruple to substitute excellencies of another kind for those which are unattainable by him, and endeavors occasionally to surpass his original, in order to make some amends for the general inferiority to which he feels that he must submit. But this would be to encourage idleness and unmanly despair. Further, it is the language of men who speak of what they do not understand; who talk of Poetry as of a matter of amusement and idle pleasure; who will converse with us as gravely about a *taste* for Poetry, as they express it, as if it were a thing as indifferent as a taste for rope-dancing, or Frontiniac or Sherry.[1] Aristotle,[2] I have been told, has said that Poetry is the most philosophic of all writing: it is so: its object is truth, not individual and local, but general, and operative; not standing upon external testimony, but carried alive into the heart by passion; truth which is its own testimony, which gives competence and confidence to the tribunal to which it appeals, and receives them from the same tribunal. Poetry is the image of man and nature. The obstacles which stand in the way of the fidelity of the Biographer and Historian, and of their consequent utility, are incalculably greater than those which are to be encountered by the Poet who comprehends the dignity of his art. The Poet writes under one restriction only, namely, the necessity of giving immediate pleasure to a human Being possessed of that information which may be expected from him, not as a lawyer, a physician, a mariner, an astronomer, or a natural philosopher, but as a Man. Except this one restriction, there is no object standing between the Poet and the image of things; between this, and the Biographer and Historian, there are a thousand.

Nor let this necessity of producing immediate pleasure be considered as a degradation of the Poet's art. It is far otherwise. It is an acknowledgment of the beauty of the universe, an acknowledgment the more sincere, because not formal, but indirect; it is a task light and easy to him who looks at the world in the spirit of love: further, it is a homage paid to the native and naked dignity of man, to the grand elementary principle of pleasure, by which he knows, and feels, and lives, and moves. We have no sympathy but what is propagated by pleasure: I would not be misunderstood; but wherever we sympathize with pain, it will be found that the sympathy is produced and carried on by subtle combinations with pleasure. We have no

---

[1] **Frontiniac** a wine made in Frontignan, France. **Sherry** a famous wine originally made near Xeres (Jerez), Spain.

[2] **Aristotle** (384-322 B.C.), the great Greek philosopher, wrote the *Poetics,* to which Wordsworth refers.

knowledge, that is, no general principles drawn from the contemplation of particular facts, but what has been built up by pleasure, and exists in us by pleasure alone. The Man of science, the Chemist and Mathematician, whatever difficulties and disgusts they may have had to struggle with, know and feel this. However painful may be the objects with which the Anatomist's knowledge is connected, he feels that his knowledge is pleasure; and where he has no pleasure he has no knowledge. What then does the Poet? He considers man and the objects that surround him as acting and reacting upon each other, so as to produce an infinite complexity of pain and pleasure; he considers man in his own nature and in his ordinary life as contemplating this with a certain quantity of immediate knowledge, with certain convictions, intuitions, and deductions, which from habit acquire the quality of intuitions; he considers him as looking upon this complex scene of ideas and sensations, and finding everywhere objects that immediately excite in him sympathies which, from the necessities of his nature, are accompanied by an over-balance of enjoyment.

To this knowledge which all men carry about with them, and to these sympathies in which, without any other discipline than that of our daily life, we are fitted to take delight, the Poet principally directs his attention. He considers man and nature as essentially adapted to each other, and the mind of man as naturally the mirror of the fairest and most interesting properties of nature. And thus the Poet, prompted by this feeling of pleasure, which accompanies him through the whole course of his studies, converses with general nature, with affections akin to those which, through labor and length of time, the Man of science has raised up in himself, by conversing with those particular parts of nature which are the objects of his studies. The knowledge both of the Poet and the Man of science is pleasure; but the knowledge of the one cleaves to us as a necessary part of our existence, our natural and unalienable inheritance; the other is a personal and individual acquisition, slow to come to us, and by no habitual and direct sympathy connecting us with our fellow-beings. The Man of science seeks truth as a remote and unknown benefactor; he cherishes and loves it in his solitude: the Poet, singing a song in which all human beings join with him, rejoices in the presence of truth as our visible friend and hourly companion. Poetry is the breath and finer spirit of all knowledge; it is the impassioned expression which is in the countenance of all science. Emphatically may it be said of the Poet, as Shakespeare hath said of man, that "he looks before and after." He is the rock of defence for human nature; an upholder and preserver, carrying everywhere with him relationship and love. In spite of difference of soil and climate, of language and manners, of laws and customs; in spite of things silently gone out of mind, and things violently destroyed; the Poet binds together by passion and knowledge the vast empire of human society, as it is spread over the whole earth, and over all time. The objects of the Poet's thoughts are everywhere; though the eyes and senses of man are, it is true, his favorite guides, yet he will follow wheresoever he can find an atmosphere of sensation in which to move his wings. Poetry is the first and last of all knowledge—it is as immortal as the heart of man. If the labors of Men of science should ever create any material revolution, direct or indirect, in our condition, and in the impressions which we habitually receive, the Poet will sleep then no more than at present; he will be ready to follow the steps of the Man of science, not only in those general indirect effects, but he will be at his side, carrying sensation into the midst of the objects of the science itself. The remotest discoveries of the Chemist, the Botanist, or Mineralogist, will be as proper objects of the Poet's art as any upon which it can be employed, if the time should ever come when these things shall be familiar to us, and the relations under which they are contemplated by the followers of these respective sciences shall be manifestly and palpably material to us as enjoying and suffering beings. If the time should ever come when what is now called science, thus familiarized to men, shall be ready to put on, as it were, a form of flesh and blood, the Poet will lend his divine spirit to aid the transfiguration, and will welcome the Being thus produced, as a dear and genuine inmate of the household of man.—It is not, then, to be supposed that any one who holds that sublime notion of Poetry which I have attempted to convey, will break in upon the sanctity and truth of his pictures by transitory and accidental ornaments, and endeavor to excite admiration of himself by arts the necessity of which must manifestly depend upon the assumed meanness of his subject.

What has been thus far said applies to Poetry in general, but especially to those parts of composition where the Poet speaks through the mouths of his characters; and upon this point it appears to authorize the conclusion that there are few persons of good sense who would not allow that the dramatic parts of composition are defective, in proportion as they deviate from the real language of nature, and are colored by a diction of the Poet's own, either peculiar to him as an individual Poet or belonging simply to Poets in general,—to a body of men who, from the circumstance of their compositions being in metre, it is expected will employ a particular language.

It is not, then, in the dramatic parts of composition that we look for this distinction of language; but still it may be proper and necessary where the Poet speaks to us in his own person and character. To this I answer by referring the Reader to the description before given of a Poet. Among the qualities there enumerated as principally conducing to form a Poet, is implied nothing differing in kind from other men, but only in degree. The sum of what was said is, that the Poet is chiefly distinguished from other men by a greater promptness to think and feel without immediate external excitement, and a greater power in expressing such thoughts and feelings as are produced in him in that manner. But these passions and thoughts and feelings are the general passions and thoughts and feelings of men. And with what are they connected? Undoubtedly with our moral sentiments and animal sensations, and with the causes which excite these; with the operations of the elements, and the appearances of the visible universe; with storm and sunshine, with the revolutions of the seasons, with cold and heat, with loss of friends and kindred, with injuries and resentments, gratitude and hope, with fear and sorrow. These, and the like, are the sensations and objects which the Poet describes, as they are the sensations of other men, and the objects which interest them. The Poet thinks and feels in the spirit of human passions. How, then, can his language differ in any material degree from that of all other men who feel vividly and see clearly? It might be *proved* that it is impossible. But supposing that this were not the case, the Poet might then be allowed to use a peculiar language when expressing his feelings for his own gratification, or that of men like himself. But Poets do not write for Poets alone, but for men. Unless, therefore, we are advocates for that admiration which subsists upon ignorance, and that pleasure which arises from hearing what we do not understand, the Poet must descend from this supposed height; and, in order to excite rational sympathy, he must express himself as other men express themselves. To this it may be added that while he is only selecting from the real language of men, or, which amounts to the same thing, composing accurately in the spirit of such selection, he is treading upon safe ground, and we know what we are to expect from him. Our feelings are the same with respect to metre; [1] for, as it may be proper to remind the Reader, the distinction of metre is regular and uniform, and not, like that which is produced by what is usually called POETIC DICTION, arbitrary, and subject to infinite caprices upon which no calculation whatever can be made. In the one case, the reader is utterly at the mercy of the Poet, respecting what imagery or diction he may choose to connect with the passion; whereas in the other, the metre obeys certain laws, to which the Poet and Reader both willingly submit because they are certain, and because no interference is made by them with the passion, but such as the concurring testimony of ages has shown to heighten and improve the pleasure which co-exists with it.

It will now be proper to answer an obvious question, namely, Why, professing these opinions, have I written in verse? To this, in addition to such answer as is included in what has been already said, I reply, in the first place, Because, however I may have restricted myself, there is still left open to me what confessedly constitutes the most valuable object of all writing, whether in prose or verse—the great and universal passions of men, the most general and interesting of their occupations, and the entire world of nature before me—to supply endless combinations of forms and imagery. Now, supposing for a moment that whatever is interesting in these objects may be as vividly described in prose, why should I be condemned for at-

[1] Here ends the passage added in 1802.

tempting to superadd to such description the charm which, by the consent of all nations, is acknowledged to exist in metrical language? To this, by such as are yet unconvinced, it may be answered that a very small part of the pleasure given by Poetry depends upon the metre, and that it is injudicious to write in metre, unless it be accompanied with the other artificial distinctions of style with which metre is usually accompanied, and that, by such deviation, more will be lost from the shock which will thereby be given to the Reader's associations than will be counterbalanced by any pleasure which he can derive from the general power of numbers. In answer to those who still contend for the necessity of accompanying metre with certain appropriate colors of style in order to the accomplishment of its appropriate end, and who also, in my opinion, greatly underrate the power of metre in itself, it might, perhaps, as far as relates to these volumes, have been almost sufficient to observe that poems are extant, written upon more humble subjects, and in a still more naked and simple style, which have continued to give pleasure from generation to generation. Now if nakedness and simplicity be a defect, the fact here mentioned affords a strong presumption that poems somewhat less naked and simple are capable of affording pleasure at the present day; and what I wished *chiefly* to attempt, at present, was to justify myself for having written under the impression of this belief.

But various causes might be pointed out why, when the style is manly, and the subject of some importance, words metrically arranged will long continue to impart such a pleasure to mankind as he who proves the extent of that pleasure will be desirous to impart. The end of poetry is to produce excitement in co-existence with an overbalance of pleasure; but, by the supposition, excitement is an unusual and irregular state of the mind; ideas and feelings do not, in that state, succeed each other in accustomed order. If the words, however, by which this excitement is produced be in themselves powerful, or the images and feelings have an undue proportion of pain connected with them, there is some danger that the excitement may be carried beyond its proper bounds. Now the co-presence of something regular, something to which the mind has been accustomed in various moods and in a less excited state, cannot but have great efficacy in tempering and restraining the passion by an intertexture of ordinary feeling, and of feeling not strictly and necessarily connected with the passion. This is unquestionably true; and hence, though the opinion will at first appear paradoxical, from the tendency of metre to divest language, in a certain degree, of its reality, and thus to throw a sort of half-consciousness of unsubstantial existence over the whole composition, there can be little doubt but that more pathetic situations and sentiments, that is, those which have a greater proportion of pain connected with them, may be endured in metrical composition, especially in rhyme, than in prose. The metre of the old ballads is very artless, yet they contain many passages which would illustrate this opinion; and, I hope, if the following poems be attentively perused, similar instances will be found in them. This opinion may be further illustrated by appealing to the Reader's own experience of the reluctance with which he comes to the reperusal of the distressful parts of *Clarissa Harlowe,* or *The Gamester,*[1] while Shakespeare's writings, in the most pathetic scenes, never act upon us, as pathetic, beyond the bounds of pleasure—an effect which, in a much greater degree than might at first be imagined, is to be ascribed to small but continual and regular impulses of pleasurable surprise from the metrical arrangement.—On the other hand (what it must be allowed will much more frequently happen), if the Poet's words should be incommensurate with the passion, and inadequate to raise the Reader to a height of desirable excitement, then (unless the Poet's choice of his metre has been grossly injudicious) in the feelings of pleasure which the Reader has been accustomed to connect with metre in general, and in the feeling, whether cheerful or melancholy, which he has been accustomed to connect with that particular movement of metre, there will be found something which will greatly contribute to impart passion to the words, and to effect the complex end which the Poet proposes to himself.

If I had undertaken a SYSTEMATIC defence of the theory here maintained, it would have been my duty to develop

[1] **Clarissa Harlowe** was a popular sentimental novel published in 1748 by Samuel Richardson. **The Gamester** was a sentimental tragedy written by Edward Moore and first produced in 1753.

the various causes upon which the pleasure received from
metrical language depends. Among the chief of these causes
is to be reckoned a principle which must be well known
to those who have made any of the Arts the object of
accurate reflection; namely, the pleasure which the mind
derives from the perception of similitude in dissimilitude.
This principle is the great spring of the activity of our
minds, and their chief feeder. From this principle the direc-
tion of the sexual appetite, and all the passions connected
with it, take their origin: it is the life of our ordinary con-
versation; and upon the accuracy with which similitude in
dissimilitude, and dissimilitude in similitude are perceived,
depend our taste and our moral feelings. It would not be a
useless employment to apply this principle to the considera-
tion of metre, and to show that metre is hence enabled to
afford much pleasure, and to point out in what manner that
pleasure is produced. But my limits will not permit me to
enter upon this subject, and I must content myself with a
general summary.

I have said that poetry is the spontaneous overflow of
powerful feelings; it takes its origin from emotion recol-
lected in tranquillity: the emotion is contemplated till, by
a species of reaction, the tranquillity gradually disappears,
and an emotion, kindred to that which was before the sub-
ject of contemplation, is gradually produced, and does itself
actually exist in the mind. In this mood successful composi-
tion generally begins, and in a mood similar to this it is
carried on; but the emotion, of whatever kind, and in what-
ever degree, from various causes, is qualified by various
pleasures, so that in describing any passions whatsoever,
which are voluntarily described, the mind will, upon the
whole, be in a state of enjoyment. If Nature be thus cautious
to preserve in a state of enjoyment a being so employed, the
Poet ought to profit by the lesson held forth to him, and
ought especially to take care that, whatever passions he
communicates to his Reader, those passions, if his Reader's
mind be sound and vigorous, should always be accom-
panied with an over-balance of pleasure. Now the music
of harmonious metrical language, the sense of difficulty
overcome, and the blind association of pleasure which has
been previously received from works of rhyme or metre of
the same or similar construction, an indistinct perception

perpetually renewed of language closely resembling that of real life, and yet, in the circumstance of metre, differing from it so widely—all these imperceptibly make up a complex feeling of delight, which is of the most important use in tempering the painful feeling always found intermingled with powerful descriptions of the deeper passions. This effect is always produced in pathetic and impassioned poetry; while in lighter compositions the ease and gracefulness with which the Poet manages his numbers are themselves confessedly a principal source of the gratification of the Reader. All that it is *necessary* to say, however, upon this subject, may be effected by affirming, what few persons will deny, that of two descriptions, either of passions, manners, or characters each of them equally well executed, the one in prose and the other in verse, the verse will be read a hundred times where the prose is read once.

Having thus explained a few of my reasons for writing in verse, and why I have chosen subjects from common life, and endeavored to bring my language near to the real language of men, if I have been too minute in pleading my own cause, I have at the same time been treating a subject of general interest; and for this reason a few words shall be added with reference solely to these particular poems, and to some defects which will probably be found in them. I am sensible that my associations must have sometimes been particular instead of general, and that, consequently, giving to things a false importance, I may have sometimes written upon unworthy subjects; but I am less apprehensive on this account, than that my language may frequently have suffered from those arbitrary connections of feelings and ideas with particular words and phrases, from which no man can altogether protect himself. Hence I have no doubt that, in some instances, feelings, even of the ludicrous, may be given to my Readers by expressions which appeared to me tender and pathetic. Such faulty expressions, were I convinced they were faulty at present, and that they must necessarily continue to be so, I would willingly take all reasonable pains to correct. But it is dangerous to make these alterations on the simple authority of a few individuals, or even of certain classes of men; for where the understanding of an author is not convinced, or his feelings altered, this cannot be done without great injury to himself:

for his own feelings are his stay and support; and, if he set them aside in one instance, he may be induced to repeat this act till his mind shall lose all confidence in itself, and become utterly debilitated. To this it may be added that the critic ought never to forget that he is himself exposed to the same errors as the Poet, and perhaps in a much greater degree: for there can be no presumption in saying of most readers that it is not probable they will be so well acquainted with the various stages of meaning through which words have passed, or with the fickleness or stability of the relations of particular ideas to each other; and, above all, since they are so much less interested in the subject, they may decide lightly and carelessly.

Long as the Reader has been detained, I hope he will permit me to caution him against a mode of false criticism which has been applied to poetry, in which the language closely resembles that of life and nature. Such verses have been triumphed over in parodies, of which Dr. Johnson's stanza is a fair specimen:—

> I put my hat upon my head
> And walked into the Strand,
> And there I met another man
> Whose hat was in his hand.

Immediately under these lines let us place one of the most justly admired stanzas of the "Babes in the Woods."

> These pretty Babes with hand in hand
> Went wandering up and down;
> But never more they saw the Man
> Approaching from the Town.

In both these stanzas the words, and the order of the words, in no respect differ from the most unimpassioned conversation. There are words in both, for example, "the Strand," and "the Town," connected with none but the most familiar ideas; yet the one stanza we admit as admirable, and the other as a fair example of the superlatively contemptible. Whence arises this difference? Not from the metre, not from the language, not from the order of the words; but the *matter* expressed in Dr. Johnson's stanza is contemptible. The proper method of treating trivial and

simple verses to which Dr. Johnson's stanza would be a
fair parallelism, is not to say, This is a bad kind of poetry,
or This is not poetry; but, This wants sense; it is neither
interesting in itself, nor can *lead* to anything interesting;
the images neither originate in that sane state of feeling
which arises out of thought, nor can excite thought or feel-
ing in the Reader. This is the only sensible manner of deal-
ing with such verses. Why trouble yourself about the species
till you have previously decided upon the genus? Why take
pains to prove that an ape is not a Newton,[1] when it is self-
evident that he is not a man?

One request I must make of my Reader, which is, that
in judging these Poems he would decide by his own feelings
genuinely, and not by reflection upon what will probably be
the judgment of others. How common is it to hear a person
say, I myself do not object to this style of composition, or
this or that expression, but to such and such classes of
people it will appear mean or ludicrous! This mode of
criticism, so destructive of all sound unadulterated judg-
ment, is almost universal: let the Reader then abide, inde-
pendently, by his own feelings, and, if he finds himself
affected, let him not suffer such conjectures to interfere
with his pleasure.

If an Author, by any single composition, has impressed
us with respect for his talents, it is useful to consider this
as affording a presumption that on other occasions, where
we have been displeased, he nevertheless may not have
written ill or absurdly; and further, to give him so much
credit for this one composition as may induce us to review
what has displeased us with more care than we should
otherwise have bestowed upon it. This is not only an act
of justice, but, in our decisions upon poetry especially, may
conduce in a high degree to the improvement of our own
taste; for an *accurate* taste in poetry, and in all the other
arts, as Sir Joshua Reynolds [2] has observed, is an *acquired*

[1] **Newton,** Sir Isaac (1642-1727) was a renowned English scientist
and philosopher who formulated the law of gravity and was cele-
brated by Wordsworth in a famous passage of *The Prelude*, Book
III, vv. 60-63.
[2] **Sir Joshua Reynolds** (1723-1792) was a distinguished English
portrait painter whose *Discourses* (annual addresses to the Royal

talent, which can only be produced by thought and a long-continued intercourse with the best models of composition. This is mentioned, not with so ridiculous a purpose as to prevent the most inexperienced Reader from judging for himself (I have already said that I wish him to judge for himself), but merely to temper the rashness of decision, and to suggest that, if Poetry be a subject on which much time has not been bestowed, the judgment may be erroneous; and that, in many cases, it necessarily will be so.

Nothing would, I know, have so effectually contributed to further the end which I have in view, as to have shown of what kind the pleasure is, and how that pleasure is produced, which is confessedly produced by metrical composition essentially different from that which I have here endeavored to recommend: for the Reader will say that he has been pleased by such composition; and what more can be done for him? The power of any art is limited; and he will suspect that, if it be proposed to furnish him with new friends, that can be only upon condition of his abandoning his old friends. Besides, as I have said, the Reader is himself conscious of the pleasure which he has received from such composition, composition to which he has peculiarly attached the endearing name of Poetry; and all men feel an habitual gratitude, and something of an honorable bigotry, for the objects which have long continued to please them: we not only wish to be pleased, but to be pleased in that particular way in which we have been accustomed to be pleased. There is in these feelings enough to resist a host of arguments; and I should be the less able to combat them successfully, as I am willing to allow that, in order entirely to enjoy the Poetry which I am recommending, it would be necessary to give up much of what is ordinarily enjoyed. But, would my limits have permitted me to point out how this pleasure is produced, many obstacles might have been removed, and the Reader assisted in perceiving that the powers of language are not so limited as he may suppose; and that it is possible for poetry to give other enjoyments, of a purer, more lasting, and more exquisite nature. This part of the subject has not been alto-

---

Academy of Arts) significantly influenced Wordsworth's critical theories.

gether neglected, but it has not been so much my present aim to prove that the interest excited by some other kinds of poetry is less vivid, and less worthy of the nobler powers of the mind, as to offer reasons for presuming that, if my purpose were fulfilled, a species of poetry would be produced which is genuine poetry, in its nature well adapted to interest mankind permanently, and likewise important in the multiplicity and quality of its moral relations.

From what has been said, and from a perusal of the Poems, the Reader will be able clearly to perceive the object which I had in view: he will determine how far it has been attained; and, what is a much more important question, whether it be worth attaining: and upon the decision of these two questions will rest my claim to the approbation of the Public.

SELECTED POEMS OF
WILLIAM WORDSWORTH

Lines

LEFT UPON A SEAT IN A YEW-TREE, WHICH STANDS NEAR
THE LAKE OF ESTHWAITE, ON A DESOLATE PART OF THE
SHORE, COMMANDING A BEAUTIFUL PROSPECT.

NAY, Traveller! rest. This lonely Yew-tree stands
Far from all human dwelling: what if here
No sparkling rivulet spread the verdant herb?
What if the bee love not these barren boughs?
Yet, if the wind breathe soft, the curling waves,
That break against the shore, shall lull thy mind
By one soft impulse saved from vacancy.
——————————Who he was
That piled these stones and with the mossy sod
First covered, and here taught this aged Tree   **10**
With its dark arms to form a circling bower,
I well remember.—He was one who owned
No common soul. In youth by science nursed,
And led by nature into a wild scene
Of lofty hopes, he to the world went forth
A favoured Being, knowing no desire
Which genius did not hallow; 'gainst the taint
Of dissolute tongues, and jealousy, and hate,
And scorn,—against all enemies prepared,
All but neglect. The world, for so it thought,   **20**
Owed him no service; wherefore he at once
With indignation turned himself away,
And with the food of pride sustained his soul
In solitude.—Stranger! these gloomy boughs
Had charms for him; and here he loved to sit,
His only visitants a straggling sheep,

The stone-chat, or the glancing sandpiper:
And on these barren rocks, with fern and heath,
And juniper and thistle, sprinkled o'er,
30　　Fixing his downcast eye, he many an hour
A morbid pleasure nourished, tracing here
An emblem of his own unfruitful life:
And, lifting up his head, he then would gaze
On the more distant scene,—how lovely 'tis
Thou seest,—and he would gaze till it became
Far lovelier, and his heart could not sustain
The beauty, still more beauteous! Nor, that time,
When nature had subdued him to herself,
Would he forget those Beings to whose minds
40　　Warm from the labours of benevolence
The world, and human life, appeared a scene
Of kindred loveliness: then he would sigh,
Inly disturbed, to think that others felt
What he must never feel: and so, lost Man!
On visionary views would fancy feed,
Till his eyes streamed with tears. In this deep vale
He died,—this seat his only monument.

If Thou be one whose heart the holy forms
Of young imagination have kept pure,
50　　Stranger! henceforth be warned; and know that pride,
Howe'er disguised in its own majesty,
Is littleness; that he who feels contempt
For any living thing, hath faculties
Which he has never used; that thought with him
Is in its infancy. The man whose eye
Is ever on himself doth look on one,
The least of Nature's works, one who might move
The wise man to that scorn which wisdom holds
Unlawful, ever. O be wiser, Thou!
60　　Instructed that true knowledge leads to love;
True dignity abides with him alone
Who, in the silent hour of inward thought,
Can still suspect, and still revere himself,
In lowliness of heart.

The Old Cumberland Beggar

I saw an aged Beggar in my walk;
And he was seated, by the highway side,
On a low structure of rude masonry
Built at the foot of a huge hill, that they
Who lead their horses down the steep rough road
May thence remount at ease. The aged Man
Had placed his staff across the broad smooth stone
That overlays the pile; and, from a bag
All white with flour, the dole of village dames,
He drew his scraps and fragments, one by one;   10
And scanned them with a fixed and serious look
Of idle computation. In the sun,
Upon the second step of that small pile,
Surrounded by those wild unpeopled hills,
He sat, and ate his food in solitude:
And ever scattered from his palsied hand,
That, still attempting to prevent the waste,
Was baffled still, the crumbs in little showers
Fell on the ground; and the small mountain birds,
Not venturing yet to peck their destined meal,   20
Approached within the length of half his staff.

Him from my childhood have I known; and then
He was so old, he seems not older now;
He travels on, a solitary Man,
So helpless in appearance, that for him
The sauntering Horseman throws not with a slack
And careless hand his alms upon the ground,
But stops,—that he may safely lodge the coin
Within the old Man's hat; nor quits him so,
But still, when he has given his horse the rein,   30
Watches the aged Beggar with a look
Sidelong, and half-reverted. She who tends
The toll-gate, when in summer at her door
She turns her wheel, if on the road she sees
The aged beggar coming, quits her work,
And lifts the latch for him that he may pass.
The post-boy, when his rattling wheels o'ertake

The aged Beggar in the woody lane,
Shouts to him from behind; and, if thus warned
40 The old man does not change his course, the boy
Turns with less noisy wheels to the roadside,
And passes gently by, without a curse
Upon his lips or anger at his heart.

He travels on, a solitary Man;
His age has no companion. On the ground
His eyes are turned, and, as he moves along,
They move along the ground; and, evermore,
Instead of common and habitual sight
Of fields with rural works, of hill and dale,
50 And the blue sky, one little span of earth
Is all his prospect. Thus, from day to day,
Bow-bent, his eyes forever on the ground,
He plies his weary journey; seeing still,
And seldom knowing that he sees, some straw,
Some scattered leaf, or marks which, in one track,
The nails of cart or chariot-wheel have left
Impressed on the white road,—in the same line,
At distance still the same. Poor Traveller!
His staff trails with him; scarcely do his feet
60 Disturb the summer dust; he is so still
In look and motion, that the cottage curs,
Ere he has passed the door, will turn away,
Weary of barking at him. Boys and girls,
The vacant and the busy, maids and youths,
And urchins newly breeched—all pass him by:
Him even the slow-paced wagon leaves behind.

But deem not this Man useless.—Statesmen! ye
Who are so restless in your wisdom, ye
Who have a broom still ready in your hands
70 To rid the world of nuisances; ye proud,
Heart-swoln, while in your pride ye contemplate
Your talents, power, or wisdom, deem him not
A burthen of the earth! 'Tis Nature's law
That none, the meanest of created things,
Of forms created the most vile and brute,
The dullest or most noxious, should exist
Divorced from good—a spirit and pulse of good,

A life and soul, to every mode of being
Inseparably linked. Then be assured
That least of all can aught—that ever owned 80
The heaven-regarding eye and front sublime
Which man is born to—sink, howe'er depressed,
So low as to be scorned without a sin;
Without offence to God cast out of view;
Like the dry remnant of a garden flower
Whose seeds are shed, or as an implement
Worn out and worthless. While from door to door,
This old Man creeps, the villagers in him
Behold a record which together binds
Past deeds and offices of charity, 90
Else unremembered, and so keeps alive
The kindly mood in hearts which lapse of years,
And that half-wisdom half-experience gives,
Make slow to feel, and by sure steps resign
To selfishness and cold oblivious cares.
Among the farms and solitary huts,
Hamlets and thinly-scattered villages,
Where'er the aged Beggar takes his rounds,
The mild necessity of use compels
To acts of love; and habit does the work 100
Of reason; yet prepares that after-joy
Which reason cherishes. And thus the soul,
By that sweet taste of pleasure unpursued,
Doth find herself insensibly disposed
To virtue and true goodness.

                  Some there are,
By their good works exalted, lofty minds,
And meditative, authors of delight
And happiness, which to the end of time
Will live, and spread, and kindle: even such minds
In childhood, from this solitary Being, 110
Or from like wanderer haply have received
(A thing more precious far than all that books
Or the solicitudes of love can do!)
That first mild touch of sympathy and thought,
In which they found their kindred with a world
Where want and sorrow were. The easy man
Who sits at his own door,—and, like the pear

That overhangs his head from the green wall,
Feeds in the sunshine; the robust and young,
120   The prosperous and unthinking, they who live
Sheltered, and flourish in a little grove
Of their own kindred;—all behold in him
A silent monitor, which on their minds
Must needs impress a transitory thought
Of self-congratulation, to the heart
Of each recalling his peculiar boons,
His charters and exemptions; and, perchance,
Though he to no one give the fortitude
And circumspection needful to preserve
130   His present blessings, and to husband up
The respite of the season, he, at least,
And 'tis no vulgar service, makes them felt.

Yet further.——Many, I believe, there are
Who live a life of virtuous decency,
Men who can hear the Decalogue and feel
No self-reproach; who of the moral law
Established in the land where they abide
Are strict observers; and not negligent
In acts of love to those with whom they dwell,
140   Their kindred, and the children of their blood.
Praise be to such, and to their slumbers peace!
—But of the poor man ask, the abject poor;
Go, and demand of him, if there be here
In this cold abstinence from evil deeds,
And these inevitable charities,
Wherewith to satisfy the human soul?
No—man is dear to man; the poorest poor
Long for some moments in a weary life
When they can know and feel that they have been,
150   Themselves, the fathers and the dealers-out
Of some small blessings; have been kind to such
As needed kindness, for this single cause,
That we have all of us one human heart.
—Such pleasure is to one kind Being known,
My neighbour, when with punctual care, each week,
Duly as Friday comes, though pressed herself

135 **Decalogue** The Ten Commandments. See Exodus, 20: 2-17

By her own wants, she from her store of meal
Takes one unsparing handful for the scrip
Of this old Mendicant, and, from her door
Returning with exhilarated heart,   160
Sits by her fire, and builds her hope in heaven.

Then let him pass, a blessing on his head!
And while in that vast solitude to which
The tide of things has borne him, he appears
To breathe and live but for himself alone,
Unblamed, uninjured, let him bear about
The good which the benignant law of Heaven
Has hung around him: and, while life is his,
Still let him prompt the unlettered villagers
To tender offices and pensive thoughts.   170
—Then let him pass, a blessing on his head!
And, long as he can wander, let him breathe
The freshness of the valleys; let his blood
Struggle with frosty air and winter snows;
And let the chartered wind that sweeps the heath
Beat his gray locks against his withered face.
Reverence the hope whose vital anxiousness
Gives the last human interest to his heart.
May never House, misnamed of Industry,
Make him a captive!—for that pent-up din,   180
Those life-consuming sounds that clog the air,
Be his the natural silence of old age!
Let him be free of mountain solitudes;
And have around him, whether heard or not,
The pleasant melody of woodland birds.
Few are his pleasures: if his eyes have now
Been doomed so long to settle upon earth
That not without some effort they behold
The countenance of the horizontal sun,
Rising or setting, let the light at least   190
Find a free entrance to their languid orbs,
And let him, *where* and *when* he will sit down
Beneath the trees, or on a grassy bank
Of highway side, and with the little birds

158 **scrip** A kind of bag or knapsack 179 **House, misnamed of
Industry** Workhouses for the poor

Share his chance-gathered meal; and, finally,
As in the eye of Nature he has lived,
So in the eye of Nature let him die!

Expostulation and Reply

"Why, William, on that old grey stone,
Thus for the length of half a day,
Why, William, sit you thus alone,
And dream your time away?

"Where are your books?—that light bequeathed
To Beings else forlorn and blind!
Up! up! and drink the spirit breathed
From dead men to their kind.

"You look round on your Mother Earth,
10   As if she for no purpose bore you;
As if you were her first-born birth,
And none had lived before you!"

One morning thus, by Esthwaite lake,
When life was sweet, I knew not why,
To me my good friend Matthew spake,
And thus I made reply:

"The eye—it cannot choose but see;
We cannot bid the ear be still;
Our bodies feel, where'er they be,
20   Against or with our will.

"Nor less I deem that there are Powers
Which of themselves our minds impress;
That we can feed this mind of ours
In a wise passiveness.

"Think you, 'mid all this mighty sum
Of things for ever speaking,
That nothing of itself will come,
But we must still be seeking?

"—Then ask not wherefore, here, alone,
Conversing as I may,   30
I sit upon this old grey stone,
And dream my time away."

The Tables Turned

AN EVENING SCENE ON THE SAME SUBJECT

Up! up! my Friend, and quit your books;
Or surely you'll grow double:
Up! up! my Friend, and clear your looks;
Why all this toil and trouble?

The sun, above the mountain's head,
A freshening lustre mellow
Through all the long green fields has spread,
His first sweet evening yellow.

Books! 'tis a dull and endless strife:
Come, hear the woodland linnet,   10
How sweet his music! on my life,
There's more of wisdom in it.

And hark! how blithe the throstle sings!
He, too, is no mean preacher:
Come forth into the light of things,
Let Nature be your Teacher.

She has a world of ready wealth,
Our minds and hearts to bless—
Spontaneous wisdom breathed by health,
Truth breathed by cheerfulness.   20

One impulse from a vernal wood
May teach you more of man,
Of moral evil and of good,
Than all the sages can.

Sweet is the lore which Nature brings;
Our meddling intellect

Mis-shapes the beauteous forms of things:—
We murder to dissect.

30   Enough of Science and of Art;
Close up those barren leaves;
Come forth, and bring with you a heart
That watches and receives.

To My Sister

IT is the first mild day of March;
Each minute sweeter than before,
The redbreast sings from the tall larch
That stands beside our door.

There is a blessing in the air,
Which seems a sense of joy to yield
To the bare trees, and mountains bare,
And grass in the green field.

My sister! ('tis a wish of mine)
10 Now that our morning meal is done,
Make haste, your morning task resign;
Come forth and feel the sun.

Edward will come with you;—and, pray,
Put on with speed your woodland dress;
And bring no book: for this one day
We'll give to idleness.

No joyless forms shall regulate
Our living calendar:
We from to-day, my Friend, will date
20 The opening of the year.

Love, now a universal birth,
From heart to heart is stealing.

13 **Edward** The young son of Basil Montagu, a Cambridge friend
of Wordsworth. Edward, whose mother died at his birth, lived
at Racedown with the Wordsworths, who received £50 a year
for his board

From earth to man, from man to earth:
—It is the hour of feeling.

One moment now may give us more
Than years of toiling reason:
Our minds shall drink at every pore
The spirit of the season.

Some silent laws our hearts will make,
Which they shall long obey: 30
We for the year to come may take
Our temper from to-day.

And from the blessed power that rolls
About, below, above,
We'll frame the measure of our souls:
They shall be tuned to love.

Then come, my Sister! come, I pray,
With speed put on your woodland dress;
And bring no book: for this one day
We'll give to idleness.   40

Lines Written in Early Spring

I HEARD a thousand blended notes,
While in a grove I sate reclined,
In that sweet mood when pleasant thoughts
Bring sad thoughts to the mind.

To her fair works did Nature link
The human soul that through me ran;
And much it grieved my heart to think
What man has made of man.

Through primrose tufts, in that green bower;
The periwinkle trailed its wreaths;   10
And 'tis my faith that every flower
Enjoys the air it breathes.

The birds around me hopped and played,
Their thoughts I cannot measure:—
But the least motion which they made,
It seemed a thrill of pleasure.

The budding twigs spread out their fan,
To catch the breezy air;
And I must think, do all I can,
20   That there was pleasure there.

If this belief from heaven be sent,
If such be Nature's holy plan,
Have I not reason to lament
What man has made of man?

Lines

COMPOSED A FEW MILES ABOVE TINTERN ABBEY, ON
REVISITING THE BANKS OF THE WYE DURING A TOUR
July 13, 1798

FIVE years have past; five summers, with the length
Of five long winters! and again I hear
These waters, rolling from their mountain-springs
With a soft inland murmur.—Once again
Do I behold these steep and lofty cliffs,
That on a wild secluded scene impress
Thoughts of more deep seclusion; and connect
The landscape with the quiet of the sky.
The day is come when I again repose
10   Here, under this dark sycamore, and view
These plots of cottage-ground, these orchard-tufts,
Which at this season, with their unripe fruits,
Are clad in one green hue, and lose themselves
'Mid groves and copses. Once again I see

22 The famous phrase, "Nature's holy plan," appeared for the
first time in the edition of 1820 *Title:* **Tintern Abbey** is a medieval
ruin in Monmouthshire on the river Wye in southwestern Eng-
land which Wordsworth first visited in 1793

These hedge-rows, hardly hedge-rows, little lines
Of sportive wood run wild: these pastoral farms,
Green to the very door; and wreaths of smoke
Sent up, in silence, from among the trees!
With some uncertain notice, as might seem
Of vagrant dwellers in the houseless woods,   20
Or of some Hermit's cave, where by his fire
The Hermit sits alone.

                    These beauteous forms,
Through a long absence, have not been to me
As is a landscape to a blind man's eye:
But oft, in lonely rooms, and 'mid the din
Of towns and cities, I have owed to them,
In hours of weariness, sensations sweet,
Felt in the blood, and felt along the heart;
And passing even into my purer mind,
With tranquil restoration:—feelings too   30
Of unremembered pleasure: such, perhaps,
As have no slight or trivial influence
On that best portion of a good man's life,
His little, nameless, unremembered, acts
Of kindness and of love. Nor less, I trust,
To them I may have owed another gift,
Of aspect more sublime; that blessed mood,
In which the burthen of the mystery,
In which the heavy and the weary weight
Of all this unintelligible world,   40
Is lightened:—that serene and blessed mood,
In which the affections gently lead us on,—
Until, the breath of this corporeal frame
And even the motion of our human blood
Almost suspended, we are laid asleep
In body, and become a living soul:
While with an eye made quiet by the power
Of harmony, and the deep power of joy,
We see into the life of things.

                        If this
Be but a vain belief, yet, oh! how oft—   50
In darkness and amid the many shapes
Of joyless daylight; when the fretful stir

Unprofitable, and the fever of the world,
Have hung upon the beatings of my heart—
How oft, in spirit, have I turned to thee,
O sylvan Wye! thou wanderer thro' the woods,
How often has my spirit turned to thee!

And now, with gleams of half-extinguished thought,
With many recognitions dim and faint,
60   And somewhat of a sad perplexity,
The picture of the mind revives again:
While here I stand, not only with the sense
Of present pleasure, but with pleasing thoughts
That in this moment there is life and food
For future years. And so I dare to hope,
Though changed, no doubt, from what I was when first
I came among these hills; when like a roe
I bounded o'er the mountains, by the sides
Of the deep rivers, and the lonely streams,
70   Wherever nature led: more like a man
Flying from something that he dreads than one
Who sought the thing he loved. For nature then
(The coarser pleasures of my boyish days,
And their glad animal movements all gone by)
To me was all in all.—I cannot paint
What then I was. The sounding cataract
Haunted me like a passion: the tall rock,
The mountain, and the deep and gloomy wood,
Their colours and their forms, were then to me
80   An appetite; a feeling and a love,
That had no need for a remoter charm,
By thought supplied, nor any interest
Unborrowed from the eye.—That time is past,
And all its aching joys are now no more,
And all its dizzy raptures. Not for this
Faint I, nor mourn nor murmur; other gifts
Have followed; for such loss, I would believe,
Abundant recompense. For I have learned
To look on nature, not as in the hour
90   Of thoughtless youth; but hearing oftentimes

86 Faint As Wordsworth uses it in this line the word means to
lose heart or courage, to become depressed and hopeless

The still, sad music of humanity,
Nor harsh nor grating, though of ample power
To chasten and subdue. And I have felt
A presence that disturbs me with the joy
Of elevated thoughts; a sense sublime
Of something far more deeply interfused,
Whose dwelling is the light of setting suns,
And the round ocean and the living air,
And the blue sky, and in the mind of man:
A motion and a spirit, that impels   100
All thinking things, all objects of all thought,
And rolls through all things. Therefore am I still
A lover of the meadows and the woods,
And mountains; and of all that we behold
From this green earth; of all the mighty world
Of eye, and ear,—both what they half create,
And what perceive; well pleased to recognise
In nature and the language of the sense
The anchor of my purest thoughts, the nurse,
The guide, the guardian of my heart, and soul   110
Of all my moral being.

                    Nor perchance,
If I were not thus taught, should I the more
Suffer my genial spirits to decay:
For thou art with me here upon the banks
Of this fair river; thou my dearest Friend,
My dear, dear Friend; and in thy voice I catch
The language of my former heart, and read
My former pleasures in the shooting lights
Of thy wild eyes. Oh! yet a little while
May I behold in thee what I was once,   120
My dear, dear Sister! and this prayer I make,
Knowing that Nature never did betray
The heart that loved her; 'tis her privilege,
Through all the years of this our life, to lead
From joy to joy: for she can so inform
The mind that is within us, so impress
With quietness and beauty, and so feed
With lofty thoughts, that neither evil tongues,

115 **dearest Friend** Wordsworth's sister Dorothy

Rash judgments, nor the sneers of selfish men,
130   Nor greetings where no kindness is, nor all
The dreary intercourse of daily life,
Shall e'er prevail against us, or disturb
Our cheerful faith, that all which we behold
Is full of blessings. Therefore let the moon
Shine on thee in thy solitary walk;
And let the misty mountain-winds be free
To blow against thee: and, in after years,
When these wild ecstasies shall be matured
Into a sober pleasure; when thy mind
140   Shall be a mansion for all lovely forms,
Thy memory be as a dwelling-place
For all sweet sounds and harmonies; oh! then,
If solitude, or fear, or pain, or grief
Should be thy portion, with what healing thoughts
Of tender joy wilt thou remember me,
And these my exhortations! Nor, perchance—
If I should be where I no more can hear
Thy voice, nor catch from thy wild eyes these gleams
Of past existence—wilt thou then forget
150   That on the banks of this delightful stream
We stood together; and that I, so long
A worshipper of Nature, hither came
Unwearied in that service: rather say
With warmer love—oh! with far deeper zeal
Of holier love. Nor wilt thou then forget
That after many wanderings, many years
Of absence, these steep woods and lofty cliffs,
And this green pastoral landscape, were to me
More dear, both for themselves and for thy sake!

A Poet's Epitaph

ART thou a Statist in the van
Of public conflicts trained and bred?
—First learn to love one living man;
Then may'st thou think upon the dead.

A Lawyer art thou?—draw not nigh!
Go, carry to some fitter place

The keenness of that practised eye,
The hardness of that sallow face.

Art thou a Man of purple cheer?
A rosy Man, right plump to see?   **10**
Approach; yet, Doctor, not too near,
This grave no cushion is for thee.

Or art thou one of gallant pride,
A Soldier and no man of chaff?
Welcome!—but lay thy sword aside,
And lean upon a peasant's staff.

Physician art thou?—one, all eyes,
Philosopher!—a fingering slave,
One that would peep and botanize
Upon his mother's grave?   **20**

Wrapt closely in thy sensual fleece,
O turn aside,—and take, I pray,
That he below may rest in peace,
Thy ever-dwindling soul, away!

A Moralist perchance appears;
Led, Heaven knows how! to this poor sod:
And he has neither eyes nor ears;
Himself his world, and his own God;

One to whose smooth-rubbed soul can cling
Nor form, nor feeling, great or small;   **30**
A reasoning, self-sufficing thing,
An intellectual All-in-all!

Shut close the door; press down the latch;
Sleep in thy intellectual crust;
Nor lose ten tickings of thy watch
Near this unprofitable dust.

But who is He, with modest looks,
And clad in homely russet brown?
He murmurs near the running brooks
A music sweeter than their own.   **40**

He is retired as noontide dew,
Or fountain in a noon-day grove;
And you must love him, ere to you
He will seem worthy of your love.

The outward shows of sky and earth,
Of hill and valley, he has viewed;
And impulses of deeper birth
Have come to him in solitude.

In common things that round us lie
Some random truths he can impart,—
The harvest of a quiet eye
That broods and sleeps on his own heart.

But he is weak; both Man and Boy,
Hath been an idler in the land;
Contented if he might enjoy
The things which others understand.

—Come hither in thy hour of strength;
Come, weak as is a breaking wave!
Here stretch thy body at full length;
Or build thy house upon this grave.

Matthew

IF Nature, for a favourite child,
In thee hath tempered so her clay,
That every hour thy heart runs wild,
Yet never once doth go astray,

Read o'er these lines; and then review
This tablet, that thus humbly rears
In such diversity of hue
Its history of two hundred years.

—When through this little wreck of fame,
Cipher and syllable! thine eye

Has travelled down to Matthew's name,
Pause with no common sympathy.

And if a sleeping tear should wake,
Then be it neither checked or stayed:
For Matthew a request I make
Which for himself he had not made.

Poor Matthew, all his frolics o'er,
Is silent as a standing pool;
Far from the chimney's merry roar,
And murmur of the village school.   20

The sighs which Matthew heaved were sighs
Of one tired out with fun and madness;
The tears which came to Matthew's eyes
Were tears of light, the dew of gladness.

Yet sometimes, when the secret cup
Of still and serious thought went round,
It seemed as if he drank it up—
He felt with spirit so profound.

—Thou soul of God's best earthly mould!
Thou happy Soul! and can it be   30
That these two words of glittering gold
Are all that must remain of thee?

Lucy Gray

OR, SOLITUDE

OFT I had heard of Lucy Gray:
And, when I crossed the wild,
I chanced to see at break of day
The solitary child.

Title: No one knows nor does it matter whether the **Lucy** of the
"Lucy" poems was a real person or a creation of Wordsworth's
imagination. She may have been Dorothy Wordsworth, Annette
Vallon, Mary Hutchinson, a combination of any two or all three
of these, or a purely literary personality. The first time Words-
worth uses the name—in a rejected fragment of "Nutting," writ-
ten in 1798—he clearly has Dorothy in mind

No mate, no comrade Lucy knew;
She dwelt on a wide moor,
—The sweetest thing that ever grew
Beside a human door!

You yet may spy the fawn at play,
The hare upon the green;
But the sweet face of Lucy Gray
Will never more be seen.

"To-night will be a stormy night—
You to the town must go;
And take a lantern, Child, to light
Your mother through the snow."

"That, Father! will I gladly do:
'Tis scarcely afternoon—
The minster-clock has just struck two,
And yonder is the moon!"

At this the Father raised his hook,
And snapped a faggot-band;
He plied his work;—and Lucy took
The lantern in her hand.

Not blither is the mountain roe:
With many a wanton stroke
Her feet disperse the powdery snow,
That rises up like smoke.

The storm came on before its time:
She wandered up and down;
And many a hill did Lucy climb:
But never reached the town.

The wretched parents all that night
Went shouting far and wide;
But there was neither sound nor sight
To serve them for a guide.

At day-break on a hill they stood
That overlooked the moor;

And thence they saw the bridge of wood,
A furlong from their door.   40

They wept—and, turning homeward, cried,
"In heaven we all shall meet;"
—When in the snow the mother spied
The print of Lucy's feet.

Then downwards from the steep hill's edge
They tracked the footmarks small;
And through the broken hawthorn hedge,
And by the long stone-wall;

And then an open field they crossed;
The marks were still the same;   50
They tracked them on, nor ever lost;
And to the bridge they came.

They followed from the snowy bank
Those footmarks, one by one,
Into the middle of the plank;
And further there were none!

—Yet some maintain that to this day
She is a living child;
That you may see sweet Lucy Gray
Upon the lonesome wild.   60

O'er rough and smooth she trips along,
And never looks behind;
And sings a solitary song
That whistles in the wind.

"Strange Fits of Passion Have I Known"

STRANGE fits of passion have I known:
And I will dare to tell,
But in the Lover's ear alone,
What once to me befell.

When she I loved looked every day
Fresh as a rose in June,
I to her cottage bent my way,
Beneath an evening-moon.

Upon the moon I fixed my eye,
All over the wide lea;
With quickening pace my horse drew nigh
Those paths so dear to me.

And now we reached the orchard-plot;
And, as we climbed the hill,
The sinking moon to Lucy's cot
Came near, and nearer still.

In one of those sweet dreams I slept,
  Kind Nature's gentlest boon!
And all the while my eyes I kept
On the descending moon.

My horse moved on; hoof after hoof
He raised, and never stopped:
When down behind the cottage roof,
At once, the bright moon dropped.

What fond and wayward thoughts will slide
Into a Lover's head!
"O mercy!" to myself I cried,
"If Lucy should be dead!"

"She Dwelt among the Untrodden Ways"

SHE dwelt among the untrodden ways
  Beside the springs of Dove,
A Maid whom there were none to praise
  And very few to love:

A violet by a mossy stone
  Half hidden from the eye!

—Fair as a star, when only one
  Is shining in the sky.

She lived unknown, and few could know
  When Lucy ceased to be;   10
But she is in her grave, and, oh,
  The difference to me!

"I Travelled among Unknown Men"

I TRAVELLED among unknown men,
  In lands beyond the sea;
Nor, England! did I know till then
  What love I bore to thee.

'Tis past, that melancholy dream!
  Nor will I quit thy shore
A second time; for still I seem
  To love thee more and more.

Among thy mountains did I feel
  The joy of my desire;   10
And she I cherished turned her wheel
  Beside an English fire.

Thy mornings showed, thy nights concealed,
  · The bowers where Lucy played;
And thine too is the last green field
  That Lucy's eyes surveyed.

"Three Years She Grew in Sun and Shower"

THREE years she grew in sun and shower,
Then Nature said, "A lovelier flower
On earth was never sown;
This Child I to myself will take;
She shall be mine, and I will make
A Lady of my own.

"Myself will to my darling be
Both law and impulse: and with me
The Girl, in rock and plain,
10   In earth and heaven, in glade and bower,
Shall feel an overseeing power
To kindle or restrain.

"She shall be sportive as the fawn
That wild with glee across the lawn
Or up the mountain springs;
And hers shall be the breathing balm,
And hers the silence and the calm
Of mute insensate things.

"The floating clouds their state shall lend
20   To her; for her the willow bend;
Nor shall she fail to see
Even in the motions of the Storm
Grace that shall mould the Maiden's form
By silent sympathy.

"The stars of midnight shall be dear
To her; and she shall lean her ear
In many a secret place
Where rivulets dance their wayward round,
And beauty born of murmuring sound
30   Shall pass into her face.

"And vital feelings of delight
Shall rear her form to stately height,
Her virgin bosom swell;
Such thoughts to Lucy I will give
While she and I together live
Here in this happy dell."

Thus Nature spake—The work was done—
How soon my Lucy's race was run!
She died, and left to me
40   This heath, this calm, and quiet scene;
The memory of what has been,
And never more will be.

"A Slumber Did My Spirit Seal"

A SLUMBER did my spirit seal;
  I had no human fears:
She seemed a thing that could not feel
  The touch of earthly years.

No motion has she now, no force;
  She neither hears nor sees;
Rolled round in earth's diurnal course,
  With rocks, and stones, and trees.

The Recluse

PART FIRST

BOOK FIRST—HOME AT GRASMERE

ONCE to the verge of yon steep barrier came
A roving school-boy; what the adventurer's age
Hath now escaped his memory—but the hour,
One of a golden summer holiday,
He well remembers, though the year be gone—
Alone and devious from afar he came;
And, with a sudden influx overpowered
At sight of this seclusion, he forgot
His haste, for hasty had his footsteps been
As boyish his pursuits; and sighing said,   **10**
"What happy fortune were it here to live!
And, if a thought of dying, if a thought
Of mortal separation, could intrude
With paradise before him, here to die!"
No Prophet was he, had not even a hope,
Scarcely a wish, but one bright pleasing thought,
A fancy in the heart of what might be
The lot of others, never could be his.

Title: **Grasmere** A town in Westmorland in or near which Words-
worth lived from December 1799 until his death in April 1850

The station whence he looked was soft and green,
20 Not giddy yet aerial, with a depth
Of vale below, a height of hills above.
For rest of body perfect was the spot,
All that luxurious nature could desire;
But stirring to the spirit; who could gaze
And not feel motions there? He thought of clouds
That sail on winds: of breezes that delight
To play on water, or in endless chase
Pursue each other through the yielding plain
Of grass or corn, over and through and through,
30 In billow after billow, evermore
Disporting—nor unmindful was the boy
Of sunbeams, shadows, butterflies and birds;
Of fluttering sylphs and softly-gliding Fays,
Genii, and winged angels that are Lords
Without restraint of all which they behold.
The illusion strengthening as he gazed, he felt
That such unfettered liberty was his,
Such power and joy; but only for this end,
To flit from field to rock, from rock to field,
40 From shore to island, and from isle to shore,
From open ground to covert, from a bed
Of meadow-flowers into a tuft of wood;
From high to low, from low to high, yet still
Within the bound of this huge concave; here
Must be his home, this valley be his world.
    Since that day forth the Place to him—*to me*
(For I who live to register the truth
Was that same young and happy Being) became
As beautiful to thought, as it had been
50 When present, to the bodily sense; a haunt
Of pure affections, shedding upon joy
A brighter joy; and through such damp and gloom
Of the gay mind, as ofttimes splenetic youth
Mistakes for sorrow, darting beams of light
That no self-cherished sadness could withstand;
And now 'tis mine, perchance for life, dear Vale,
Beloved Grasmere (let the wandering streams
Take up, the cloud-capt hills repeat, the Name)
One of thy lowly Dwellings is my Home.
60   And was the cost so great? and could it seem

An act of courage, and the thing itself
A conquest? who must bear the blame? Sage man
Thy prudence, thy experience, thy desires,
Thy apprehensions—blush thou for them all.
   Yes the realities of life so cold,
So cowardly, so ready to betray,
So stinted in the measure of their grace
As we pronounce them, doing them much wrong,
Have been to me more bountiful than hope,
Less timid than desire—but that is past.   70
   On Nature's invitation do I come,
By Reason sanctioned. Can the choice mislead,
That made the calmest, fairest spot of earth
With all its unappropriated good
My own; and not mine only, for with me
Entrenched, say rather peacefully embowered,
Under yon orchard, in yon humble cot,
A younger Orphan of a home extinct,
The only Daughter of my Parents dwells.
   Ay, think on that, my heart, and cease to stir,   80
Pause upon that and let the breathing frame
No longer breathe, but all be satisfied.
—Oh, if such silence be not thanks to God
For what hath been bestowed, then where, where then
Shall gratitude find rest? Mine eyes did ne'er
Fix on a lovely object, nor my mind
Take pleasure in the midst of happy thoughts,
But either She whom now I have, who now
Divides with me this loved abode, was there
Or not far off. Where'er my footsteps turned,   90
Her voice was like a hidden Bird that sang.
The thought of her was like a flash of light,
Or an unseen companionship, a breath
Of fragrance independent of the Wind.
In all my goings, in the new and old
Of all my meditations, and in this
Favourite of all, in this the most of all.
—What being, therefore, since the birth of Man
Had ever more abundant cause to speak
Thanks, and if favors of the Heavenly Muse   100
Make him more thankful, then to call on Verse
To aid him and in song resound his joy?

The boon is absolute; surpassing grace
To me hath been vouchsafed; among the bowers
Of blissful Eden this was neither given
Nor could be given, possession of the good
Which had been sighed for, ancient thought fulfilled,
And dear Imagination realized,
Up to their highest measure, yea and more.
110   Embrace me then, ye Hills, and close me in;
Now in the clear and open day I feel
Your guardianship; I take it to my heart;
'Tis like the solemn shelter of the night.
But I would call thee beautiful, for mild,
And soft, and gay, and beautiful thou art,
Dear Valley, having in thy face a smile,
Though peaceful, full of gladness. Thou art pleased,
Pleased with thy crags and woody steeps, thy Lake,
Its one green island and its winding shores;
120   The multitude of little rocky hills,
Thy Church and cottages of mountain stone
Clustered like stars some few, but single most,
And lurking dimly in their shy retreats,
Or glancing at each other cheerful looks
Like separated stars with clouds between.
What want we? have we not perpetual streams,
Warm woods, and sunny hills, and fresh green fields,
And mountains not less green, and flocks and herds,
And thickets full of songsters, and the voice
130   Of lordly birds, an unexpected sound
Heard now and then from morn to latest eve,
Admonishing the man who walks below
Of solitude and silence in the sky?
These have we, and a thousand nooks of earth
Have also these, but nowhere else is found,
Nowhere (or is it fancy?) can be found
The one sensation that is here; 't is here,
Here as it found its way into my heart
In childhood, here as it abides by day,
140   By night, here only; or in chosen minds
That take it with them hence, where'er they go.
—'T is, but I cannot name it, 't is the sense
Of majesty, and beauty, and repose,
A blended holiness of earth and sky,

Something that makes this individual spot,
This small abiding-place of many men,
A termination, and a last retreat,
A center, come from wheresoe'er you will,
A whole without dependence or defect,
Made for itself, and happy in itself,   150
Perfect contentment, Unity entire.

   Bleak season was it, turbulent and bleak,
When hitherward we journeyed side by side
Through burst of sunshine and through flying showers;
Paced the long vales—how long they were—and yet
How fast that length of way was left behind,
Wensley's rich Vale, and Sedbergh's naked heights.
The frosty wind, as if to make amends
For its keen breath, was aiding to our steps,
And drove us onward like two ships at sea,   160
Or like two birds, companions in mid-air,
Parted and reunited by the blast.

   Stern was the face of nature; we rejoiced
In that stern countenance, for our souls thence drew
A feeling of their strength. The naked trees,
The icy brooks, as on we passed, appeared
To question us. "Whence come ye, to what end?"
They seemed to say. "What would ye," said the shower,
"Wild Wanderers, whither through my dark domain?"
The sunbeam said, "Be happy." When this vale   170
We entered, bright and solemn was the sky
That faced us with a passionate welcoming,
And led us to our threshold. Daylight failed
Insensibly, and round us gently fell
Composing darkness, with a quiet load
Of full contentment, in a little shed
Disturbed, uneasy in itself as seemed,
And wondering at its new inhabitants.
It loves us now, this Vale so beautiful
Begins to love us! by a sullen storm,   180
Two months unwearied of severest storm,

152 Wordsworth and Dorothy left Sockburn on 17 December
1799, passed through Wensley and Sedbergh (on one day they
walked twenty-one miles), and arrived at Grasmere on 20
December

It put the temper of our minds to proof,
And found us faithful through the gloom, and heard
The poet mutter his prelusive songs
With cheerful heart, an unknown voice of joy
Among the silence of the woods and hills;
Silent to any gladsomeness of sound
With all their shepherds.

But the gates of Spring
Are opened; churlish winter hath given leave
190 That she should entertain for this one day,
Perhaps for many genial days to come,
His guests, and make them jocund.—They are pleased,
But most of all the birds that haunt the flood,
With the mild summons; inmates though they be
Of Winter's household, they keep festival
This day, who drooped, or seemed to droop, so long;
They show their pleasure, and shall I do less?
Happier of happy though I be, like them
I cannot take possession of the sky,
200 Mount with a thoughtless impulse, and wheel there
One of a mighty multitude, whose way
Is a perpetual harmony and dance
Magnificent. Behold how with a grace
Of ceaseless motion, that might scarcely seem
Inferior to angelical, they prolong
Their curious pastime, shaping in mid-air,
And sometimes with ambitious wing that soars
High as the level of the mountain tops,
A circuit ampler than the lake beneath,
210 Their own domain;—but ever, while intent
On tracing and retracing that large round,
Their jubilant activity evolves
Hundreds of curves and circlets, to and fro,
Upwards and downwards; progress intricate
Yet unperplexed, as if one spirit swayed
Their indefatigable flight. 'T is done,
Ten times and more I fancied it had ceased,
But lo! the vanished company again
Ascending, they approach. I hear their wings
220 Faint, faint at first; and then an eager sound
Passed in a moment—and as faint again!
They tempt the sun to sport among their plumes;

Tempt the smooth water, or the gleaming ice,
To show them a fair image,—'t is themselves,
Their own fair forms upon the glimmering plain
Painted more soft and fair as they descend,
Almost to touch,—then up again aloft,
Up with a sally and a flash of speed,
As if they scorned both resting-place and rest!
—This day is a thanksgiving, 'tis a day   230
Of glad emotion and deep quietness;
Not upon me alone hath been bestowed,
Me rich in many onward-looking thoughts,
The penetrating bliss; oh surely these
Have felt it, not the happy choirs of spring,
Her own peculiar family of love
That sport among green leaves, a blither train!
   But two are missing, two, a lonely pair
Of milk-white Swans; wherefore are they not seen
Partaking this day's pleasure? From afar   240
They came, to sojourn here in solitude,
Choosing this Valley, they who had the choice
Of the whole world. We saw them day by day,
Through those two months of unrelenting storm,
Conspicuous at the centre of the Lake
Their safe retreat, we knew them well, I guess
That the whole valley knew them; but to us
They were more dear than may be well believed,
Not only for their beauty, and their still
And placid way of life, and constant love   250
Inseparable, not for these alone,
But that *their* state so much resembled ours,
They having also chosen this abode;
They strangers, and we strangers, they a pair,
And we a solitary pair like them.
They should not have departed; many days
Did I look forth in vain, nor on the wing
Could see them, nor in that small open space
Of blue unfrozen water, where they lodged
And lived so long in quiet, side by side.   260
Shall we behold them consecrated friends,
Faithful companions, yet another year
Surviving, they for us, and we for them,
And neither pair be broken? nay perchance

It is too late already for such hope;
The Dalesmen may have aimed the deadly tube,
And parted them; or haply both are gone
One death, and that were mercy given to both.
Recall, my song, the ungenerous thought; forgive,
270 Thricefavoured Region, the conjecture harsh
Of such inhospitable penalty
Inflicted upon confidence so pure.
Ah! if I wished to follow where the sight
Of all that is before my eyes, the voice
Which speaks from a presiding spirit here,
Would lead me, I should whisper to myself:
They who are dwellers in this holy place
Must needs themselves be hallowed, they require
No benediction from the stranger's lips,
280 For they are blessed already; none would give
The greeting "peace be with you" unto them,
For peace they have; it cannot but be theirs,
And mercy, and forbearance—nay—not these—
Their healing offices a pure good-will
Precludes, and charity beyond the bounds
Of charity—an overflowing love;
Not for the creature only, but for all
That is around them; love for everything
Which in their happy Region they behold!
290   Thus do we soothe ourselves, and when the thought
Is passed, we blame it not for having come.
—What if I floated down a pleasant stream,
And now am landed, and the motion gone,
Shall I reprove myself? Ah no, the stream
Is flowing, and will never cease to flow,
And I shall float upon that stream again.
By such forgetfulness the soul becomes,
Words cannot say how beautiful: then hail,
Hail to the visible Presence, hail to thee,
300 Delightful Valley, habitation fair!
And to whatever else of outward form
Can give an inward help, can purify,
And elevate, and harmonize, and soothe,
And steal away, and for a while deceive
And lap in pleasing rest, and bear us on
Without desire in full complacency,

Contemplating perfection absolute,
And entertained as in a placid sleep.
  But not betrayed by tenderness of mind
That feared, or wholly overlooked the truth,   **310**
Did we come hither, with romantic hope
To find in midst of so much loveliness
Love, perfect love: of so much majesty
A like majestic frame of mind in those
Who here abide, the persons like the place.
Not from such hope, or aught of such belief,
Hath issued any portion of the joy
Which I have felt this day. An awful voice
'Tis true hath in my walks been often heard,
Sent from the mountains or the sheltered fields,   **320**
Shout after shout—reiterated whoop,
In manner of a bird that takes delight
In answering to itself: or like a hound
Single at chase among the lonely woods,
His yell repeating; yet it was in truth
A human voice—a spirit of coming night;
How solemn when the sky is dark, and earth
Not dark, nor yet enlightened, but by snow
Made visible, amid a noise of winds
And bleatings manifold of mountain sheep,   **330**
Which in that iteration recognize
Their summons, and are gathering round for food,
Devoured with keenness, ere to grove or bank
Or rocky bield with patience they retire.
  That very voice, which, in some timid mood
Of superstitious fancy, might have seemed
Awful as ever stray demoniac uttered,
His steps to govern in the wilderness;
Or as the Norman Curfew's regular beat
To hearths when first they darkened at the knell: **340**
That shepherd's voice, it may have reached mine ear
Debased and under profanation, made
The ready organ of articulate sounds
From ribaldry, impiety, or wrath,
Issuing when shame hath ceased to check the brawls
Of some abused Festivity—so be it.
I came not dreaming of unruffled life,
Untainted manners; born among the hills,

Bred also there, I wanted not a scale
350   To regulate my hopes; pleased with the good
I shrink not from the evil with disgust,
Or with immoderate pain. I look for Man,
The common creature of the brotherhood,
Differing but little from the Man elsewhere,
For selfishness and envy and revenge,
Ill neighbourhood—pity that this should be—
Flattery and double-dealing, strife and wrong.
   Yet is it something gained, it is in truth
A mighty gain, that Labour here preserves
360   His rosy face, a servant only here
Of the fireside or of the open field,
A Freeman therefore sound and unimpaired:
That extreme penury is here unknown,
And cold and hunger's abject wretchedness
Mortal to body and the heaven-born mind:
That they who want are not too great a weight
For those who can relieve; here may the heart
Breathe in the air of fellow-suffering
Dreadless, as in a kind of fresher breeze
370   Of her own native element, the hand
Be ready and unwearied without plea,
From tasks too frequent or beyond its power,
For languor or indifference or despair.
And as these lofty barriers break the force
Of winds,—this deep Vale, as it doth in part
Conceal us from the storm, so here abides
A power and a protection for the mind,
Dispensed indeed to other solitudes
Favored by noble privilege like this,
380   Where kindred independence of estate
Is prevalent, where he who tills the field,
He, happy man! is master of the field,
And treads the mountains which his Fathers trod.
   Not less than halfway up yon mountain's side,
Behold a dusky spot, a grove of Firs.
That seems still smaller than it is; this grove
Is haunted—by what ghost? a gentle spirit
Of memory faithful to the call of love;
For, as reports the Dame, whose fire sends up
390   Yon curling smoke from the grey cot below,

The trees (her first-born child being then a babe)
Were planted by her husband and herself,
That ranging o'er the high and houseless ground
Their sheep might neither want from perilous storm
Of winter, nor from summer's sultry heat,
A friendly covert; "and they knew it well,"
Said she, "for thither as the trees grew up
We to the patient creatures carried food
In times of heavy snow." She then began
In fond obedience to her private thoughts   400
To speak of her dead husband; is there not
An art, a music, and a strain of words
That shall be life, the acknowledged voice of life,
Shall speak of what is done among the fields,
Done truly there, or felt, of solid good
And real evil, yet be sweet withal,
More grateful, more harmonious than the breath,
The idle breath of softest pipe attuned
To pastoral fancies? Is there such a stream
Pure and unsullied flowing from the heart   410
With motions of true dignity and grace?
Or must we seek that stream where Man is not?
Methinks I could repeat in tuneful verse,
Delicious as the gentlest breeze that sounds
Through the aerial fir-grove—could preserve
Some portion of its human history
As gathered from the Matron's lips, and tell
Of tears that have been shed at sight of it,
And moving dialogues between this Pair
Who in their prime of wedlock, with joint hands   420
Did plant the grove, now flourishing, while they
No longer flourish, he entirely gone,
She withering in her loneliness. Be this
A task above my skill—the silent mind
Has her own treasures, and I think of these,
Love what I see, and honour humankind.
   No, we are not alone, we do not stand,
My sister here misplaced and desolate,
Loving what no one cares for but ourselves.
We shall not scatter through the plains and rocks 430
Of this fair Vale, and o'er its spacious heights,
Unprofitable kindliness, bestowed

On objects unaccustomed to the gifts
Of feeling, which were cheerless and forlorn
But few weeks past, and would be so again
Were we not here; we do not tend a lamp
Whose lustre we alone participate,
Which shines dependent upon us alone,
Mortal though bright, a dying, dying flame.
440   Look where we will, some human hand has been
Before us with its offering; not a tree
Sprinkles these little pastures, but the same
Hath furnished matter for a thought; perchance
For some one serves as a familiar friend.
Joy spreads, and sorrow spreads; and this whole Vale
Home of untutored shepherds as it is,
Swarms with sensation, as with gleams of sunshine,
Shadows or breezes, scents or sounds. Nor deem
These feelings, though subservient more than ours
450   To every day's demand for daily bread,
And borrowing more their spirit and their shape
From self-respecting interests; deem them not
Unworthy therefore, and unhallowed—no,
They lift the animal being, do themselves
By nature's kind and ever-present aid
Refine the selfishness from which they spring,
Redeem by love the individual sense
Of anxiousness, with which they are combined.
And thus it is that fitly they become
460   Associates in the joy of purest minds:
They blend therewith congenially: meanwhile
Calmly they breathe their own undying life
Through this their mountain sanctuary; long
Oh long may it remain inviolate,
Diffusing health and sober cheerfulness,
And giving to the moments as they pass
Their little boons of animating thought
That sweeten labour, make it seen and felt
To be no arbitrary weight imposed,
470   But a glad function natural to man.
    Fair proof of this, newcomer though I be,
Already have I gained; the inward frame,
Though slowly opening, opens every day
With process not unlike to that which cheers

A pensive stranger journeying at his leisure
Through some Helvetian Dell; when low-hung mists
Break up and are beginning to recede;
How pleased he is where thin and thinner grows
The veil, or where it parts at once, to spy
The dark pines thrusting forth their spiky heads;   480
To watch the spreading lawns with cattle grazed;
Then to be greeted by the scattered huts
As they shine out; and *see* the streams whose murmur
Had soothed his ear while *they* were hidden; how pleased
To have about him which way e'er he goes
Something on every side concealed from view,
In every quarter something visible
Half seen or wholly, lost and found again,
Alternate progress and impediment,
And yet a growing prospect in the main.   490
    Such pleasure now is mine, albeit forced,
Herein less happy than the Traveller,
To cast from time to time a painful look
Upon unwelcome things which unawares
Reveal themselves, not therefore is my heart
Depressed, nor does it fear what is to come;
But confident, enriched at every glance,
The more I see the more delight my mind
Receives, or by reflection can create:
Truth justifies herself, and as she dwells   500
With Hope, who would not follow where she leads?
    Nor let me pass unheeded other loves
Where no fear is, and humbler sympathies.
Already hath sprung up within my heart
A liking for the small grey horse that bears
The paralytic man, and for the brute
In Scripture sanctified—the patient brute
On which the cripple, in the quarry maimed,
Rides to and fro: I know them and their ways.
The famous sheep-dog, first in all the vale,   510
Though yet to me a stranger, will not be
A stranger long; nor will the blind man's guide,
Meek and neglected thing, of no renown!
Soon will peep forth the primrose, ere it fades
Friends shall I have at dawn, blackbird and thrush

476 **Helvetian** Swiss

To rouse me, and a hundred warblers more!
And if those Eagles to their ancient hold
Return, Helvellyn's Eagles! with the Pair
From my own door I shall be free to claim
520 Acquaintance, as they sweep from cloud to cloud.
The owl that gives the name to Owlet-Crag
Have I heard whooping, and he soon will be
A chosen one of my regards. See there
The heifer in yon little croft belongs
To one who holds it dear; with duteous care
She reared it, and in speaking of her charge
I heard her scatter some endearing words
Domestic, and in spirit motherly,
She being herself a mother; happy Beast,
530 If the caresses of a human voice
Can make it so, and care of human hands.
    And ye as happy under Nature's care,
Strangers to me and all men, or at least
Strangers to all particular amity,
All intercourse of knowledge or of love
That parts the individual from his kind.
Whether in large communities ye keep
From year to year, not shunning man's abode,
A settled residence, or be from far
540 Wild creatures, and of many homes, that come
The gift of winds, and whom the winds again
Take from us at your pleasure; yet shall ye
Not want for this your own subordinate place
In my affections. Witness the delight
With which erewhile I saw that multitude
Wheel through the sky, and see them now at rest,
Yet not at rest upon the glassy lake:
They *cannot* rest—they gambol like young whelps;
Active as lambs, and overcome with joy
550 They try all frolic motions; flutter, plunge,
And beat the passive water with their wings.
Too distant are they for plain view, but lo!
Those little fountains, sparkling in the sun,
Betray their occupation, rising up
First one and then another silver spout,
As one or other takes the fit of glee,
Fountains and spouts, yet somewhat in the guise

Of plaything fireworks, that on festal nights
Sparkle about the feet of wanton boys.
—How vast the compass of this theatre, 560
Yet nothing to be seen but lovely pomp
And silent majesty; the birch-tree woods
Are hung with thousand thousand diamond drops
Of melted hoar-frost, every tiny knot
In the bare twigs, each little budding-place
Cased with its several beads; what myriads these
Upon one tree, while all the distant grove,
That rises to the summit of the steep,
Shows like a mountain built of silver light:
See yonder the same pageant, and again 570
Behold the universal imagery
Inverted, all its sun-bright features touched
As with the varnish and the gloss of dreams.
Dreamlike the blending also of the whole
Harmonious landscape: all along the shore
The boundary lost—the line invisible
That parts the image from reality;
And the clear hills, as high as they ascend
Heavenward, so deep piercing the lake below.
Admonished of the days of love to come 580
The raven croaks, and fills the upper air
With a strange sound of genial harmony;
And in and all about that playful band,
Incapable although they be of rest,
And in their fashion very rioters,
There is a stillness; and they seem to make
Calm revelry in that their calm abode.
Them leaving to their joyous hours I pass,
Pass with a thought the life of the whole year
That is to come: the throng of woodland flowers 590
And lilies that will dance upon the waves.

  Say boldly then that solitude is not
Where these things are: he truly is alone,
He of the multitude whose eyes are doomed
To hold a vacant commerce day by day
With Objects wanting life—repelling love;
He by the vast metropolis immured,
Where pity shrinks from unremitting calls,
Where numbers overwhelm humanity,

600 And neighbourhood serves rather to divide
Than to unite—what sighs more deep than his,
Whose nobler will hath long been sacrificed;
Who must inhabit under a black sky
A city, where, if indifference to disgust
Yield not to scorn or sorrow, living men
Are ofttimes to their fellow-men no more
Than to the forest Hermit are the leaves
That hang aloft in myriads; nay, far less,
For they protect his walk from sun and shower,
610 Swell his devotion with their voice in storms,
And whisper while the stars twinkle among them
His lullaby. From crowded streets remote,
Far from the living and dead Wilderness
Of the thronged world, Society is here
A true community—a genuine frame
Of many into one incorporate.
That must be looked for here: paternal sway,
One household, under God, for high and low,
One family and one mansion; to themselves
620 Appropriate, and divided from the world,
As if it were a cave, a multitude
Human and brute, possessors undisturbed
Of this Recess—their legislative Hall,
Their Temple, and their glorious Dwelling-place.
    Dismissing therefore all Arcadian dreams,
All golden fancies of the golden age,
The bright array of shadowy thoughts from times
That were before all time, or are to be
Ere time expire, the pageantry that stirs
630 Or will be stirring, when our eyes are fixed
On lovely objects, and we wish to part
With all remembrance of a jarring world,
—Take we at once this one sufficient hope,
What need of more? that we shall neither droop
Nor pine for want of pleasure in the life
Scattered about us, nor through want of aught
That keeps in health the insatiable mind.
—That we shall have for knowledge and for love
Abundance, and that feeling as we do
640 How goodly, how exceeding fair, how pure
From all reproach is yon ethereal vault,

And this deep Vale, its earthly counterpart,
By which and under which we are enclosed
To breathe in peace; we shall moreover find
(If sound, and what we ought to be ourselves,
If rightly we observe and justly weigh)
The inmates not unworthy of their home,
The Dwellers of their Dwelling.
                              And if this
Were otherwise, we have within ourselves
Enough to fill the present day with joy,   **650**
And overspread the future years with hope,
Our beautiful and quiet home, enriched
Already with a stranger whom we love
Deeply, a stranger of our Father's house,
A never-resting Pilgrim of the Sea,
Who finds at last an hour to his content
Beneath our roof. And others whom we love
Will seek us also, Sisters of our hearts,
And one, like them, a Brother of our hearts,
Philosopher and Poet, in whose sight   **660**
These mountains will rejoice with open joy.
—Such is our wealth! O Vale of Peace we are
And must be, with God's will, a happy Band.
   Yet 't is not to enjoy that we exist,
For that end only; something must be done:
I must not walk in unreproved delight
These narrow bounds, and think of nothing more,
No duty that looks further, and no care.
Each Being has his office, lowly some
And common, yet all worthy if fulfilled   **670**
With zeal, acknowledgment that with the gift
Keeps pace a harvest answering to the seed.
Of ill-advised Ambition and of Pride
I would stand clear, but yet to me I feel
That an internal brightness is vouchsafed
That must not die, that must not pass away.
Why does this inward lustre fondly seek
And gladly blend with outward fellowship?
Why do *they* shine around me whom I love?

655 **Stranger** Wordsworth's brother John, captain of the East
Indiaman, *Earl of Abergavenny* 657 **Others** Mary and Sara
Hutchinson 659 **One** Coleridge

680 Why do they teach me, whom I thus revere?
Strange question, yet it answers not itself.
That humble Roof embowered among the trees,
That calm fireside, it is not even in them,
Blest as they are, to furnish a reply
That satisfies and ends in perfect rest.
Possessions have I that are solely mine,
Something within which yet is shared by none,
Not even the nearest to me and most dear,
Something which power and effort may impart;
690 I would impart it, I would spread it wide:
Immortal in the world which is to come—
Forgive me if I add another claim—
And would not wholly perish even in this,
Lie down and be forgotten in the dust,
I and the modest Partners of my days
Making a silent company in death;
Love, knowledge, all my manifold delights,
All buried with me without monument
Or profit unto any but ourselves!
700 It must not be, if I, divinely taught,
Be privileged to speak as I have felt
Of what in man is human or divine.
     While yet an innocent little one, with a heart
That doubtless wanted not its tender moods,
I breathed (for this I better recollect)
Among wild appetites and blind desires,
Motions of savage instinct my delight
And exaltation. Nothing at that time
So welcome, no temptation half so dear
710 As that which urged me to a daring feat,
Deep pools, tall trees, black chasms, and dizzy crags,
And tottering towers: I loved to stand and read
Their looks forbidding, read and disobey,
Sometimes in act and evermore in thought.
With impulses, that scarcely were by these
Surpassed in strength, I heard of danger met
Or sought with courage; enterprise forlorn
By one, sole keeper of his own intent,
Or by a resolute few, who for the sake
720 Of glory fronted multitudes in arms.
Yea, to this hour I cannot read a Tale

Of two brave vessels matched in deadly fight,
And fighting to the death, but I am pleased
More than a wise man ought to be; I wish,
Fret, burn, and struggle, and in soul am there.
But me hath Nature tamed, and bade to seek
For other agitations, or be calm;
Hath dealt with me as with a turbulent stream,
Some nursling of the mountains which she leads
Through quiet meadows, after he has learnt   730
His strength, and had his triumph and his joy,
His desperate course of tumult and of glee.
That which in stealth by Nature was performed
Hath Reason sanctioned: her deliberate Voice
Hath said; be mild, and cleave to gentle things,
Thy glory and thy happiness be there.
Nor fear, though thou confide in me, a want
Of aspirations that have been—of foes
To wrestle with, and victory to complete,
Bounds to be leapt, darkness to be explored;   740
All that inflamed thy infant heart, the love,
The longing, the contempt, the undaunted quest,
All shall survive, though changed their office, all
Shall live, it is not in their power to die.
      Then farewell to the Warrior's Schemes, farewell
The forwardness of soul which looks that way
Upon a less incitement than the Cause
Of Liberty endangered, and farewell
That other hope, long mine, the hope to fill
The heroic trumpet with the Muse's breath!   750
Yet in this peaceful Vale we will not spend
Unheard-of days, though loving peaceful thought,
A voice shall speak, and what will be the theme?
      On Man, on Nature, and on Human Life,
Musing in solitude, I oft perceive
Fair trains of imagery before me rise,
Accompanied by feelings of delight
Pure, or with no unpleasing sadness mixed;
And I am conscious of affecting thoughts
And dear remembrances, whose presence soothes   760
Or elevates the mind, intent to weigh
The good and evil of our mortal state.
—To these emotions, whencesoe'er they come,

Whether from breath of outward circumstance,
Or from the Soul—an impulse to herself—
I would give utterance in numerous verse.
Of Truth, of Grandeur, Beauty, Love, and Hope,
And melancholy Fear subdued by Faith;
Of blessèd consolation in distress;
770 Of moral strength, and intellectual Power;
Of joy in widest commonalty spread;
Of the individual Mind that keeps her own
Inviolate retirement, subject there
To Conscience only, and the law supreme
Of that Intelligence which governs all—
I sing:—"fit audience let me find though few!"
    So prayed, more gaining than he asked, the Bard—
In holiest mood. Urania, I shall need
Thy guidance, or a greater Muse, if such
780 Descend to earth or dwell in highest heaven!
For I must tread on shadowy ground, must sink
Deep—and, aloft ascending, breathe in worlds
To which the heaven of heavens is but a veil.
All strength—all terror, single or in bands,
That ever was put forth in personal form—
Jehovah—with his thunder, and the choir
Of shouting Angels, and the empyreal thrones—
I pass them unalarmed. Not Chaos, not
The darkest pit of lowest Erebus,
790 Nor aught of blinder vacancy, scooped out
By help of dreams—can breed such fear and awe
As fall upon us often when we look
Into our Minds, into the Mind of Man—
My haunt, and the main region of my song
—Beauty—a living Presence of the earth,
Surpassing the most fair ideal Forms
Which craft of delicate Spirits hath composed
From earth's materials—waits upon my steps;
Pitches her tents before me as I move,

777 **Bard** John Milton. The quotation in the preceding line is from *Paradise Lost*, VII, 31 778 **Urania** The classical Muse of Astronomy who was adopted and invoked by Milton in *Paradise Lost* as the source of divine inspiration 789 **Erebus** Variously the son of Chaos and a region of uttermost darkness through which the dead must pass on their way to hell

An hourly neighbour. Paradise, and groves   800
Elysian, Fortunate Fields—like those of old
Sought in the Atlantic Main—why should they be
A history only of departed things,
Or a mere fiction of what never was?
For the discerning intellect of Man,
When wedded to this goodly universe
In love and holy passion, shall find these
A simple produce of the common day.
—I, long before the blissful hour arrives,
Would chant, in lonely peace, the spousal verse   810
Of this great consummation:—and, by words
Which speak of nothing more than what we are,
Would I arouse the sensual from their sleep
Of Death, and win the vacant and the vain
To noble raptures; while my voice proclaims
How exquisitely the individual Mind
(And the progressive powers perhaps no less
Of the whole species) to the external World
Is fitted;—and how exquisitely, too—
Theme this but little heard of among men—   820
The external World is fitted to the Mind;
And the creation (by no lower name
Can it be called) which they with blended might
Accomplish:—this is our high argument.
—Such grateful haunts forgoing, if I oft
Must turn elsewhere—to travel near the tribes
And fellowships of men, and see ill sights
Of madding passions mutually inflamed;
Must hear Humanity in fields and groves
Pipe solitary anguish; or must hang   830
Brooding above the fierce confederate storm
Of sorrow, barricadoed evermore
Within the walls of cities—may these sounds
Have their authentic comment; that even these
Hearing, I be not downcast or forlorn!—
Descend, prophetic Spirit! that inspir'st
The human Soul of universal earth,
Dreaming on things to come; and dost possess

801 **Elysian, Fortunate Fields** Imaginary regions in Greek myth-
ology, supposedly located in the Atlantic Ocean west of Gibraltar,
and inhabited after death by the souls of the blessed

A metropolitan temple in the hearts
840 Of mighty Poets; upon me bestow
A gift of genuine insight; that my Song
With star-like virtue in its place may shine,
Shedding benignant influence, and secure
Itself from all malevolent effect
Of those mutations that extend their sway
Throughout the nether sphere!—And if with this
I mix more lowly matter; with the thing
Contemplated, describe the mind and Man
Contemplating; and who, and what he was—
850 The transitory Being that beheld
This Vision;—when and where and how he lived;
Be not his labor useless. If such theme
May sort with highest objects, then—dread Power!
Whose gracious favour is the primal source
Of all illumination—may my Life
Express the image of a better time,
More wise desires, and simpler manners;—nurse
My Heart in genuine freedom:—all pure thoughts
Be with me;—so shall thy unfailing love
860 Guide, and support, and cheer me to the end!

Michael

A PASTORAL POEM

If from the public way you turn your steps
Up the tumultuous brook of Green-head Ghyll,
You will suppose that with an upright path
Your feet must struggle; in such bold ascent
The pastoral mountains front you, face to face.
But, courage! for around that boisterous brook
The mountains have all opened out themselves,
And made a hidden valley of their own.
No habitation can be seen; but they
10 Who journey thither find themselves alone
With a few sheep, with rocks and stones, and kites
That overhead are sailing in the sky.
It is in truth an utter solitude;

Nor should I have made mention of this Dell
But for one object which you might pass by,
Might see and notice not. Beside the brook
Appears a straggling heap of unhewn stones!
And to that simple object appertains
A story—unenriched with strange events,
Yet not unfit, I deem, for the fireside,   20
Or for the summer shade. It was the first
Of those domestic tales that spake to me
Of Shepherds, dwellers in the valleys, men
Whom I already loved;—not verily
For their own sakes, but for the fields and hills
Where was their occupation and abode.
And hence this Tale, while I was yet a Boy
Careless of books, yet having felt the power
Of Nature, by the gentle agency
Of natural objects, led me on to feel   30
For passions that were not my own, and think
(At random and imperfectly indeed)
On man, the heart of man, and human life.
Therefore, although it be a history
Homely and rude, I will relate the same
For the delight of a few natural hearts;
And, with yet fonder feeling, for the sake
Of youthful Poets, who among these hills
Will be my second self when I am gone.

    Upon the forest-side in Grasmere Vale   40
There dwelt a Shepherd, Michael was his name;
An old man, stout of heart, and strong of limb.
His bodily frame had been from youth to age
Of an unusual strength: his mind was keen,
Intense, and frugal, apt for all affairs,
And in his shepherd's calling he was prompt
And watchful more than ordinary men.
Hence had he learned the meaning of all winds,
Of blasts of every tone; and oftentimes,
When others heeded not, he heard the South   50
Make subterraneous music, like the noise
Of bagpipers on distant Highland hills.
The Shepherd, at such warning, of his flock
Bethought him, and he to himself would say,

"The winds are now devising work for me!"
And, truly, at all times, the storm, that drives
The traveller to a shelter, summoned him
Up to the mountains: he had been alone
Amid the heart of many thousand mists,
60   That came to him, and left him, on the heights.
So lived he till his eightieth year was past.
And grossly that man errs, who should suppose
That the green valleys, and the streams and rocks,
Were things indifferent to the Shepherd's thoughts.
Fields, where with cheerful spirits he had breathed
The common air; hills, which with vigorous step
He had so often climbed; which had impressed
So many incidents upon his mind
Of hardship, skill or courage, joy or fear;
70   Which, like a book, preserved the memory
Of the dumb animals, whom he had saved,
Had fed or sheltered, linking to such acts
The certainty of honourable gain;
Those fields, those hills—what could they less? had laid
Strong hold on his affections, were to him
A pleasurable feeling of blind love,
The pleasure which there is in life itself.

His days had not been passed in singleness.
His Helpmate was a comely matron, old—
80   Though younger than himself full twenty years.
She was a woman of a stirring life,
Whose heart was in her house: two wheels she had
Of antique form, this large, for spinning wool;
That small, for flax; and, if one wheel had rest,
It was because the other was at work.
The Pair had but one inmate of their house,
An only Child, who had been born to them
When Michael, telling o'er his years, began
To deem that he was old,—in shepherd's phrase,
90   With one foot in the grave. This only Son,
With two brave sheep-dogs tried in many a storm,
The one of an inestimable worth,
Made all their household. I may truly say,
That they were as a proverb in the vale
For endless industry. When day was gone,

And from their occupations out of doors
The Son and Father were come home, even then,
Their labour did not cease; unless when all
Turned to the cleanly supper-board, and there,
Each with a mess of pottage and skimmed milk,   100
Sat round the basket piled with oaten cakes,
And their plain home-made cheese. Yet when the meal
Was ended, Luke (for so the Son was named)
And his old Father both betook themselves
To such convenient work as might employ
Their hands by the fire-side; perhaps to card
Wool for the Housewife's spindle, or repair
Some injury done to sickle, flail, or scythe,
Or other implement of house or field.

    Down from the ceiling, by the chimney's edge,   110
That in our ancient uncouth country style
With huge and black projection overbrowed
Large space beneath, as duly as the light
Of day grew dim the Housewife hung a lamp;
An aged utensil, which had performed
Service beyond all others of its kind.
Early at evening did it burn—and late,
Surviving comrade of uncounted hours,
Which, going by from year to year, had found,
And left, the couple neither gay perhaps   120
Nor cheerful, yet with objects and with hopes,
Living a life of eager industry.
And now, when Luke had reached his eighteenth year,
There by the light of this old lamp they sate,
Father and Son, while far into the night
The Housewife plied her own peculiar work,
Making the cottage through the silent hours
Murmur as with the sound of summer flies.
This light was famous in its neighbourhood,
And was a public symbol of the life   130
That thrifty Pair had lived. For, as it chanced,
Their cottage on a plot of rising ground
Stood single, with large prospect, north and south,
High into Easedale, up to Dunmail-Raise,
And westward to the village near the lake;
And from this constant light, so regular,

And so far seen, the House itself, by all
Who dwelt within the limits of the vale,
Both old and young, was named THE EVENING STAR.

140   Thus living on through such a length of years,
The Shepherd, if he loved himself, must needs
Have loved his Helpmate; but to Michael's heart
This son of his old age was yet more dear—
Less from instinctive tenderness, the same
Fond spirit that blindly works in the blood of all—
Than that a child, more than all other gifts
That earth can offer to declining man,
Brings hope with it, and forward-looking thoughts,
And stirrings of inquietude, when they
150   By tendency of nature needs must fail.
Exceeding was the love he bare to him,
His heart and his heart's joy! For oftentimes
Old Michael, while he was a babe in arms,
Had done him female service, not alone
For pastime and delight, as is the use
Of fathers, but with patient mind enforced
To acts of tenderness; and he had rocked
His cradle, as with a woman's gentle hand.

And in a later time, ere yet the Boy
160   Had put on boy's attire, did Michael love,
Albeit of a stern unbending mind,
To have the Young-one in his sight, when he
Wrought in the field, or on his shepherd's stool
Sate with a fettered sheep before him stretched
Under the large old oak, that near his door
Stood single, and, from matchless depth of shade,
Chosen for the Shearer's covert from the sun,
Thence in our rustic dialect was called
The CLIPPING TREE, a name which yet it bears.
170   There, while they two were sitting in the shade,
With others round them, earnest all and blithe,
Would Michael exercise his heart with looks
Of fond correction and reproof bestowed
Upon the Child, if he disturbed the sheep
By catching at their legs, or with his shouts
Scared them, while they lay still beneath the shears.

And when by Heaven's good grace the boy grew up
A healthy Lad, and carried in his cheek
Two steady roses that were five years old;
Then Michael from a winter coppice cut   180
With his own hand a sapling, which he hooped
With iron, making it throughout in all
Due requisites a perfect shepherd's staff,
And gave it to the Boy; wherewith equipt
He as a watchman oftentimes was placed
At gate or gap, to stem or turn the flock;
And, to his office prematurely called,
There stood the urchin, as you will divine,
Something between a hindrance and a help;
And for this cause not always, I believe,   190
Receiving from his Father hire of praise;
Though nought was left undone which staff, or voice,
Or looks, or threatening gestures, could perform.

But soon as Luke, full ten years old, could stand
Against the mountain blasts; and to the heights,
Nor fearing toil, nor length of weary ways,
He with his Father daily went, and they
Were as companions, why should I relate
That objects which the Shepherd loved before
Were dearer now? that from the Boy there came   200
Feelings and emanations—things which were
Light to the sun and music to the wind;
And that the old Man's heart seemed born again?

Thus in his Father's sight the Boy grew up:
And now, when he had reached his eighteenth year,
He was his comfort and his daily hope.

While in this sort the simple household lived
From day to day, to Michael's ear there came
Distressful tidings. Long before the time
Of which I speak, the Shepherd had been bound   210
In surety for his brother's son, a man
Of an industrious life, and ample means;
But unforeseen misfortunes suddenly
Had prest upon him; and old Michael now
Was summoned to discharge the forfeiture,

A grievous penalty, but little less
Than half his substance. This unlooked-for claim,
At the first hearing, for a moment took
More hope out of his life than he supposed
220 That any old man ever could have lost.
As soon as he had armed himself with strength
To look his trouble in the face, it seemed
The Shepherd's sole resource to sell at once
A portion of his patrimonial fields.
Such was his first resolve; he thought again,
And his heart failed him. "Isabel," said he,
Two evenings after he had heard the news,
"I have been toiling more than seventy years,
And in the open sunshine of God's love
230 Have we all lived; yet, if these fields of ours
Should pass into a stranger's hand, I think
That I could not lie quiet in my grave.
Our lot is a hard lot; the sun himself
Has scarcely been more diligent than I;
And I have lived to be a fool at last
To my own family. An evil man
That was, and made an evil choice, if he
Were false to us; and, if he were not false,
There are ten thousand to whom loss like this
240 Had been no sorrow. I forgive him;—but
'Twere better to be dumb than to talk thus.

    When I began, my purpose was to speak
Of remedies and of a cheerful hope.
Our Luke shall leave us, Isabel; the land
Shall not go from us, and it shall be free;
He shall possess it, free as is the wind
That passes over it. We have, thou know'st,
Another kinsman—he will be our friend
In this distress. He is a prosperous man,
250 Thriving in trade—and Luke to him shall go,
And with his kinsman's help and his own thrift
He quickly will repair this loss, and then
He may return to us. If here he stay,
What can be done? Where every one is poor,
What can be gained?"
                    At this the old Man paused,
And Isabel sat silent, for her mind

Was busy, looking back into past times.
There's Richard Bateman, thought she to herself,
He was a parish-boy—at the church-door
They made a gathering for him, shillings, pence,   260
And halfpennies, wherewith the neighbours bought
A basket, which they filled with pedlar's wares;
And, with this basket on his arm, the lad
Went up to London, found a master there,
Who, out of many, chose the trusty boy
To go and overlook his merchandise
Beyond the seas; where he grew wondrous rich,
And left estates and monies to the poor,
And, at his birth-place, built a chapel floored
With marble, which he sent from foreign lands.   270
These thoughts, and many others of like sort,
Passed quickly through the mind of Isabel,
And her face brightened. The old Man was glad,
And thus resumed:—"Well, Isabel! this scheme
These two days has been meat and drink to me.
Far more than we have lost is left us yet.

We have enough—I wish indeed that I
Were younger;—but this hope is a good hope.
Make ready Luke's best garments, of the best
Buy for him more, and let us send him forth   280
To-morrow, or the next day, or to-night:
    If he *could* go, the Boy should go tonight."

Here Michael ceased, and to the fields went forth
With a light heart. The Housewife for five days
Was restless morn and night, and all day long
Wrought on with her best fingers to prepare
Things needful for the journey of her son.
But Isabel was glad when Sunday came
To stop her in her work: for, when she lay
By Michael's side, she through the last two nights   290
Heard him, how he was troubled in his sleep:
And when they rose at morning she could see
That all his hopes were gone. That day at noon
She said to Luke, while they two by themselves
Were sitting at the door, "Thou must not go:
We have no other Child but thee to lose,
None to remember—do not go away,

For if thou leave thy Father he will die."
The Youth made answer with a jocund voice;
300 And Isabel, when she had told her fears,
Recovered heart. That evening her best fare
Did she bring forth, and all together sat
Like happy people round a Christmas fire.

With daylight Isabel resumed her work;
And all the ensuing week the house appeared
As cheerful as a grove in Spring: at length
The expected letter from their kinsman came,
With kind assurances that he would do
His utmost for the welfare of the Boy;
310 To which, requests were added, that forthwith
He might be sent to him. Ten times or more
The letter was read over; Isabel
Went forth to show it to the neighbours round;
Nor was there at that time on English land
A prouder heart than Luke's. When Isabel
Had to her house returned, the old Man said,
"He shall depart to-morrow." To this word
The Housewife answered, talking much of things
Which, if at such short notice he should go,
320 Would surely be forgotten. But at length
She gave consent, and Michael was at ease.

Near the tumultuous brook of Green-head Ghyll,
In that deep valley, Michael had designed
To build a Sheep-fold; and, before he heard
The tidings of his melancholy loss,
For this same purpose he had gathered up
A heap of stones, which by the streamlet's edge
Lay thrown together, ready for the work.
With Luke that evening thitherward he walked;
330 And soon as they had reached the place he stopped,
And thus the old Man spake to him:—"My son,
Tomorrow thou wilt leave me: with full heart
I look upon thee, for thou art the same
That wert a promise to me ere thy birth,
And all thy life hast been my daily joy.
I will relate to thee some little part
Of our two histories; 'twill do thee good

When thou art from me, even if I should touch
On things thou canst not know of.—After thou
First cam'st into the world—as oft befalls   340
To new-born infants—thou didst sleep away
Two days, and blessings from thy Father's tongue
Then fell upon thee. Day by day passed on,
And still I loved thee with increasing love.
Never to living ear came sweeter sounds
Than when I heard thee by our own fireside
First uttering, without words, a natural tune;
While thou, a feeding babe, didst in thy joy
Sing at thy Mother's breast. Month followed month,
And in the open fields my life was passed   350
And on the mountains; else I think that thou
Hadst been brought up upon thy Father's knees.
But we were playmates, Luke: among these hills,
As well thou knowest, in us the old and young
Have played together, nor with me didst thou
Lack any pleasure which a boy can know."
Luke had a manly heart; but at these words
He sobbed aloud. The old Man grasped his hand,
And said, "Nay, do not take it so—I see
That these are things of which I need not speak.   360
—Even to the utmost I have been to thee
A kind and a good Father: and herein
I but repay a gift which I myself
Received at others' hands; for, though now old
Beyond the common life of man, I still
Remember them who loved me in my youth.
Both of them sleep together: here they lived,
As all their Forefathers had done; and, when
At length their time was come, they were not loth
To give their bodies to the family mould.   370
I wished that thou shouldst live the life they lived,
But 'tis a long time to look back, my Son,
And see so little gain from threescore years.
These fields were burthened when they came to me;
Till I was forty years of age, not more
Than half of my inheritance was mine.
I toiled and toiled; God blessed me in my work,
And till these three weeks past the land was free.
—It looks as if it never could endure

380 Another Master. Heaven forgive me, Luke,
    If I judge ill for thee, but it seems good
    That thou shouldst go."
                      At this the old Man paused;
    Then, pointing to the stones near which they stood,
    Thus, after a short silence, he resumed:
    "This was a work for us; and now, my Son,
    It is a work for me. But, lay one stone—
    Here, lay it for me, Luke, with thine own hands.
    Nay, Boy, be of good hope;—we both may live
    To see a better day. At eighty-four
390 I still am strong and hale;—do thou thy part;
    I will do mine.—I will begin again
    With many tasks that were resigned to thee:
    Up to the heights, and in among the storms,
    Will I without thee go again, and do
    All works which I was wont to do alone,
    Before I knew thy face.—Heaven bless thee, Boy!
    Thy heart these two weeks has been beating fast
    With many hopes; it should be so—yes—yes—
    I knew that thou couldst never have a wish
400 To leave me, Luke: thou hast been bound to me
    Only by links of love: when thou art gone,
    What will be left to us!—But I forget
    My purposes. Lay now the corner-stone,
    As I requested; and hereafter, Luke,
    When thou art gone away, should evil men
    Be thy companions, think of me, my Son,
    And of this moment; hither turn thy thoughts,
    And God will strengthen thee: amid all fear
    And all temptation, Luke, I pray that thou
410 May'st bear in mind the life thy Fathers lived,
    Who, being innocent, did for that cause
    Bestir them in good deeds. Now, fare thee well—
    When thou return'st, thou in this place wilt see
    A work which is not here: a covenant
    'Twill be between us; but, whatever fate
    Befall thee, I shall love thee to the last,
    And bear thy memory with me to the grave."

    The Shepherd ended here; and Luke stooped down,
    And, as his Father had requested, laid

The first stone of the Sheep-fold. At the sight   **420**
The old Man's grief broke from him; to his heart
He pressed his Son, he kissèd him and wept;
And to the house together they returned.
—Hushed was that House in peace, or seeming peace
Ere the night fell:—with morrow's dawn the Boy
Began his journey, and, when he had reached
The public way, he put on a bold face;
And all the neighbours, as he passed their doors,
Came forth with wishes and with farewell prayers,
That followed him till he was out of sight.   **430**

   A good report did from their Kinsman come,
Of Luke and his well-doing: and the Boy
Wrote loving letters, full of wondrous news,
Which, as the Housewife phrased it, were throughout
"The prettiest letters that were ever seen."
Both parents read them with rejoicing hearts.
So, many months passed on: and once again
The Shepherd went about his daily work
With confident and cheerful thoughts; and now
Sometimes when he could find a leisure hour   **440**
He to that valley took his way, and there
Wrought at the Sheep-fold. Meantime Luke began
To slacken in his duty; and, at length,
He in the dissolute city gave himself
To evil courses: ignominy and shame
Fell on him, so that he was driven at last
To seek a hiding-place beyond the seas.

   There is a comfort in the strength of love;
'Twill make a thing endurable, which else
Would overset the brain, or break the heart: **450**
I have conversed with more than one who well
Remember the old Man, and what he was
Years after he had heard this heavy news.
His bodily frame had been from youth to age
Of an unusual strength. Among the rocks
He went, and still looked up to sun and cloud,
And listened to the wind; and, as before,
Performed all kinds of labour for his sheep,
And for the land, his small inheritance.

460 And to that hollow dell from time to time
Did he repair, to build the Fold of which
His flock had need. 'Tis not forgotten yet
The pity which was then in every heart
For the old Man—and 'tis believed by all
That many and many a day he thither went,
And never lifted up a single stone.

There, by the Sheep-fold, sometimes was he seen
Sitting alone, or with his faithful Dog,
Then old, beside him, lying at his feet.
470 The length of full seven years, from time to time,
He at the building of this Sheep-fold wrought,
And left the work unfinished when he died.
Three years, or little more, did Isabel
Survive her Husband: at her death the estate
Was sold, and went into a stranger's hand.
The Cottage which was named the EVENING STAR
Is gone—the ploughshare has been through the ground
On which it stood; great changes have been wrought
In all the neighbourhood:—yet the oak is left
480 That grew beside their door; and the remains
Of the unfinished Sheep-fold may be seen
Beside the boisterous brook of Green-head Ghyll.

To the Cuckoo

O Blithe New-comer! I have heard,
I hear thee and rejoice.
O Cuckoo! shall I call thee Bird,
Or but a wandering Voice?

While I am lying on the grass
Thy twofold shout I hear;
From hill to hill it seems to pass
At once far off, and near.

Though babbling only to the Vale,
10 Of sunshine and of flowers,

Thou bringest unto me a tale
Of visionary hours.

Thrice welcome, darling of the Spring!
Even yet thou art to me
No bird, but an invisible thing,
A voice, a mystery;

The same whom in my schoolboy days
I listened to; that Cry
Which made me look a thousand ways
In bush, and tree, and sky.   20

To seek thee did I often rove
Through woods and on the green;
And thou wert still a hope, a love;
Still longed for, never seen.

And I can listen to thee yet;
Can lie upon the plain
And listen, till I do beget
That golden time again.

O blessèd Bird! the earth we pace
Again appears to be   30
An unsubstantial, faery place;
That is fit home for Thee!

Resolution and Independence

I

THERE was a roaring in the wind all night;
The rain came heavily and fell in floods;
But now the sun is rising calm and bright;
The birds are singing in the distant woods;
Over his own sweet voice the Stock-dove broods;
The Jay makes answer as the Magpie chatters;
And all the air is filled with pleasant noise of waters.

II

All things that love the sun are out of doors;
The sky rejoices in the morning's birth;
10 The grass is bright with rain-drops;—on the moors
The hare is running races in her mirth;
And with her feet she from the plashy earth
Raises a mist; that, glittering in the sun,
Runs with her all the way, wherever she doth run.

III

I was a Traveller then upon the moor;
I saw the hare that raced about with joy;
I heard the woods and distant waters roar;
Or heard them not, as happy as a boy:
The pleasant season did my heart employ:
20 My old remembrances went from me wholly;
And all the ways of men, so vain and melancholy.

IV

But, as it sometimes chanceth, from the might
Of joy in minds that can no further go,
As high as we have mounted in delight
In our dejection do we sink as low;
To me that morning did it happen so;
And fears and fancies thick upon me came;
Dim sadness—and blind thoughts, I knew not, nor could
    name.

V

I heard the sky-lark warbling in the sky;
30 And I bethought me of the playful hare:
Even such a happy Child of earth am I;
Even as these blissful creatures do I fare;
Far from the world I walk, and from all care;
But there may come another day to me—
Solitude, pain of heart, distress, and poverty.

VI

My whole life I have lived in pleasant thought,
As if life's business were a summer mood;
As if all needful things would come unsought

To genial faith, still rich in genial good;
But how can He expect that others should   **40**
Build for him, sow for him, and at his call
Love him, who for himself will take no heed at all?

VII

I thought of Chatterton, the marvellous Boy,
The sleepless Soul that perished in his pride;
Of Him who walked in glory and in joy
Following his plough, along the mountain-side:
By our own spirits are we deified:
We Poets in our youth begin in gladness;
But thereof come in the end despondency and madness.

VIII

Now, whether it were by peculiar grace,   **50**
A leading from above, a something given,
Yet it befell that, in this lonely place,
When I with these untoward thoughts had striven,
Beside a pool bare to the eye of heaven
I saw a Man before me unawares:
The oldest man he seemed that ever wore grey hairs.

IX

As a huge stone is sometimes seen to lie
Couched on the bald top of an eminence;
Wonder to all who do the same espy,
By what means it could thither come, and whence;   **60**
So that it seems a thing endued with sense:
Like a sea-beast crawled forth, that on a shelf
Of rock or sand reposeth, there to sun itself;

X

Such seemed this Man, not all alive nor dead,
Nor all asleep—in his extreme old age:
His body was bent double, feet and head

43 **Chatterton** Thomas Chatterton (1752-1770) was a young poet
of promise from Bristol who wrote excellent spurious medieval
poems which he attributed to an imaginary fifteenth-century
monk named Thomas Rowley. Chatterton killed himself with ar-
senic at the age of seventeen 45 Robert Burns (1759-1796)

Coming together in life's pilgrimage;
As if some dire constraint of pain, or rage
Of sickness felt by him in times long past,
70 A more than human weight upon his frame had cast.

XI

Himself he propped, limbs, body, and pale face,
Upon a long grey staff of shaven wood:
And, still as I drew near with gentle pace,
Upon the margin of that moorish flood
Motionless as a cloud the old Man stood,
That heareth not the loud winds when they call;
And moveth all together, if it move at all.

XII

At length, himself unsettling, he the pond
Stirred with his staff, and fixedly did look
80 Upon the muddy water, which he conned,
As if he had been reading in a book:
And now a stranger's privilege I took;
And, drawing to his side, to him did say,
"This morning gives us promise of a glorious day."

XIII

A gentle answer did the old Man make,
In courteous speech which forth he slowly drew:
And him with further words I thus bespake,
"What occupation do you there pursue?
This is a lonesome place for one like you."
90 Ere he replied, a flash of mild surprise
Broke from the sable orbs of his yet-vivid eyes.

XIV

His words came feebly, from a feeble chest,
But each in solemn order followed each,
With something of a lofty utterance drest—
Choice word and measured phrase, above the reach
Of ordinary men; a stately speech;
Such as grave Livers do in Scotland use,
Religious men, who give to God and man their dues.

XV

He told, that to these waters he had come
To gather leeches, being old and poor: 100
Employment hazardous and wearisome!
And he had many hardships to endure:
From pond to pond he roamed, from moor to moor;
Housing, with God's good help, by choice or chance;
And in this way he gained an honest maintenance.

XVI

The old Man still stood talking by my side;
But now his voice to me was like a stream
Scarce heard; nor word from word could I divide;
And the whole body of the Man did seem
Like one whom I had met with in a dream;   110
Or like a man from some far region sent,
To give me human strength, by apt admonishment.

XVII

My former thoughts returned: the fear that kills;
And hope that is unwilling to be fed;
Cold, pain, and labour, and all fleshly ills;
And mighty Poets in their misery dead.
—Perplexed, and longing to be comforted,
My question eagerly did I renew,
"How is it that you live, and what is it you do?"

XVIII

He with a smile did then his words repeat;   120
And said that, gathering leeches, far and wide
He travelled; stirring thus about his feet
The waters of the pools where they abide.
"Once I could meet with them on every side;
But they have dwindled long by slow decay;
Yet still I persevere, and find them where I may."

100 A leech is a blood-sucking worm some two or three inches
in length. In Wordsworth's day the European fresh-water variety
was extensively used by physicans for bleeding patients

XIX

While he was talking thus, the lonely place,
The old Man's shape, and speech—all troubled me:
In my mind's eye I seemed to see him pace
130 About the weary moors continually,
Wandering about alone and silently.
While I these thoughts within myself pursued,
He, having made a pause, the same discourse renewed.

XX

And soon with this he other matter blended,
Cheerfully uttered, with demeanour kind,
But stately in the main; and, when he ended,
I could have laughed myself to scorn to find
In that decrepit Man so firm a mind.
"God," said I, "be my help and stay secure;
140 I'll think of the Leech-gatherer on the lonely moor!"

SONNETS

ON THE EXTINCTION OF THE
VENETIAN REPUBLIC

Once did She hold the gorgeous east in fee;
And was the safeguard of the west: the worth
Of Venice did not fall below her birth,
Venice, the eldest Child of Liberty.
She was a maiden City, bright and free;
No guile seduced, no force could violate;
And, when she took unto herself a Mate,
She must espouse the everlasting Sea.
And what if she had seen those glories fade,
Those titles vanish, and that strength decay;   **10**
Yet shall some tribute of regret be paid
When her long life hath reached its final day:
Men are we, and must grieve when even the Shade
Of that which once was great is passed away.

Title: To Wordsworth, Venice, along with Switzerland and
England, was a symbol of the historic cause of liberty pitted
against tyrannical power. After 1177, when the Venetians de-
feated the German Emperor in a naval encounter, a ring was
cast into the sea each year with great ceremony to signify the
wedding of the Doge to the Adriatic, of which he was clearly
master. During the Middle Ages and the early years of the
Renaissance Venice was pre-eminent commercially and as a
naval power in the Mediterranean. In 1797 Napoleon con-
quered Venice and divided her territory between France and
Austria

COMPOSED UPON WESTMINSTER BRIDGE

September 3, 1802

EARTH has not anything to show more fair:
Dull would he be of soul who could pass by
A sight so touching in its majesty:
This City now doth, like a garment, wear
The beauty of the morning; silent, bare,
Ships, towers, domes, theatres, and temples lie
Open unto the fields, and to the sky;
All bright and glittering in the smokeless air.
Never did sun more beautifully steep
10   In his first splendour, valley, rock, or hill;
Ne'er saw I, never felt, a calm so deep!
The river glideth at his own sweet will:
Dear God! the very houses seem asleep;
And all that mighty heart is lying still!

"IT IS A BEAUTEOUS EVENING, CALM AND FREE"

IT is a beauteous evening, calm and free,
The holy time is quiet as a Nun
Breathless with adoration; the broad sun
Is sinking down in its tranquillity;
The gentleness of heaven broods o'er the Sea:
20   Listen! the mighty Being is awake,
And doth with his eternal motion make
A sound like thunder—everlastingly.
Dear Child! dear Girl! that walkest with me here,
If thou appear untouched by solemn thought,
Thy nature is not therefore less divine:
Thou liest in Abraham's bosom all the year;
And worshipp'st at the Temple's inner shrine,
God being with thee when we know it not.

23 **Dear Child!** The child here referred to was Caroline, the natural daughter of Wordsworth and Annette Vallon. When the sonnet was composed Caroline was not quite ten years old

IN LONDON

September, 1802

O Friend! I know not which way I must look
For comfort, being, as I am, opprest,
To think that now our life is only drest
For show; mean handy-work of craftsman, cook,
Or groom!—We must run glittering like a brook
In the open sunshine, or we are unblest:
The wealthiest man among us is the best:
No grandeur now in nature or in book
Delights us. Rapine, avarice, expense,
This is idolatry; and these we adore: 10
Plain living and high thinking are no more:
The homely beauty of the good old cause
Is gone; our peace, our fearful innocence,
And pure religion breathing household laws.

LONDON

1802

MILTON! thou shouldst be living at this hour:
England hath need of thee: she is a fen
Of stagnant waters: altar, sword, and pen,
Fireside, the heroic wealth of hall and bower,
Have forfeited their ancient English dower   20
Of inward happiness. We are selfish men;
Oh! raise us up, return to us again;
And give us manners, virtue, freedom, power.
Thy soul was like a Star, and dwelt apart;
Thou hadst a voice whose sound was like the sea:
Pure as the naked heavens, majestic, free,
So didst thou travel on life's common way,
In cheerful godliness; and yet thy heart
The lowliest duties on herself did lay.

"GREAT MEN HAVE BEEN AMONG US"

GREAT men have been among us; hands that penned
And tongues that uttered wisdom—better none:
The later Sidney, Marvel, Harrington,
Young Vane, and others who called Milton friend.
These moralists could act and comprehend:
They knew how genuine glory was put on;
Taught us how rightfully a nation shone
In splendour: what strength was, that would not bend
But in magnanimous meekness. France, 't is strange,
10 Hath brought forth no such souls as we had then.
Perpetual emptiness! unceasing change!
No single volume paramount, no code,
No master spirit, no determined road;
But equally a want of books and men!

TO TOUSSAINT L'OUVERTURE

TOUSSAINT, the most unhappy man of men!
Whether the whistling Rustic tend his plough
Within thy hearing, or thy head be now
Pillowed in some deep dungeon's earless den;—
O miserable Chieftain! where and when
20 Wilt thou find patience? Yet die not; do thou
Wear rather in thy bonds a cheerful brow:
Though fallen thyself, never to rise again,
Live, and take comfort. Thou hast left behind
Powers that will work for thee; air, earth, and skies;
There's not a breathing of the common wind
That will forget thee; thou hast great allies;
Thy friends are exultations, agonies,
And love, and man's unconquerable mind.

3-4 **Sidney, Marvel, Harrington . . . Vane** These Englishmen were heroically active in the establishment of the Puritan Commonwealth, as well as champions of the republican principles which Wordsworth, more than a century later, admired and endorsed *Title:* **Toussaint L'Ouverture** (1743-1803) was a Negro revolutionist on the island of Haiti, whose independence from Napoleon and France he declared in 1801. Overcome by a French force, Toussaint was thrown into prison, where he died several months after Wordsworth wrote this sonnet

"ENGLAND! THE TIME HAS COME WHEN THOU SHOULD'ST WEAN"

ENGLAND! the time has come when thou should'st wean
Thy heart from its emasculating food;
The truth should now be better understood;
Old things have been unsettled; we have seen
Fair seed-time, better harvest might have been
But for thy trespasses; and, at this day,
If for Greece, Egypt, India, Africa,
Aught good were destined, thou would'st step between.
England! all nations in this charge agree:
But worse, more ignorant in love and hate,   10
Far—far more abject, is thine Enemy:
Therefore the wise pray for thee, though the freight
Of thy offences be a heavy weight:
Oh grief that Earth's best hopes rest all with Thee!

"IT IS NOT TO BE THOUGHT OF THAT THE FLOOD"

IT is not to be thought of that the Flood
Of British freedom, which, to the open sea
Of the world's praise, from dark antiquity
Hath flowed, "with pomp of waters unwithstood,"
Roused though it be full often to a mood
Which spurns the check of salutary bands,   20
That this most famous Stream in bogs and sands
Should perish; and to evil and to good
Be lost for ever. In our halls is hung
Armoury of the invincible Knights of old:
We must be free or die, who speak the tongue
That Shakespeare spake; the faith and morals hold
Which Milton held.—In every thing we are sprung
Of Earth's first blood, have titles manifold.

18 Quoted from **Civil Wars**, I, 7, by Samuel Daniel, an Eliza-
bethan of whose poetry Wordsworth was particularly fond

"THE WORLD IS TOO MUCH WITH US; LATE AND SOON"

THE world is too much with us; late and soon,
Getting and spending, we lay waste our powers:
Little we see in Nature that is ours;
We have given our hearts away, a sordid boon!
This Sea that bares her bosom to the moon;
The winds that will be howling at all hours,
And are up-gathered now like sleeping flowers;
For this, for everything, we are out of tune;
It moves us not.—Great God! I'd rather be
10   A Pagan suckled in a creed outworn;
So might I, standing on this pleasant lea,
Have glimpses that would make me less forlorn;
Have sight of Proteus rising from the sea;
Or hear old Triton blow his wreathèd horn.

THOUGHT OF A BRITON ON THE SUBJUGATION OF SWITZERLAND

Two Voices are there; one is of the sea,
One of the mountains; each a mighty Voice:
In both from age to age thou didst rejoice,
They were thy chosen music, Liberty!
There came a Tyrant, and with holy glee
20   Thou fought'st against him; but hast vainly striven:
Thou from thy Alpine holds at length art driven,
Where not a torrent murmurs heard by thee.
Of one deep bliss thy ear hath been bereft:
Then cleave, O cleave to that which still is left;
For, high-souled Maid, what sorrow would it be
That Mountain floods should thunder as before,
And Ocean bellow from his rocky shore,
And neither awful Voice be heard by thee!

13 **Proteus** was a Greek sea god who possessed prophetic power and the ability to assume different shapes 14 **Triton** Another sea god, half man and half fish, usually represented as blowing on a conch-shell trumpet 15 **Two Voices** England and Switzerland 19 **Tyrant** Napoleon

"NUNS FRET NOT AT THEIR CONVENT'S NARROW ROOM"

Nuns fret not at their convent's narrow room;
And hermits are contented with their cells;
And students with their pensive citadels;
Maids at the wheel, the weaver at his loom,
Sit blithe and happy; bees that soar for bloom,
High as the highest Peak of Furness-fells,
Will murmur by the hour in foxglove bells:
In truth the prison, unto which we doom
Ourselves, no prison is: and hence for me,
In sundry moods, 'twas pastime to be bound   10
Within the Sonnet's scanty plot of ground;
Pleased if some Souls (for such there needs must be)
Who have felt the weight of too much liberty,
Should find brief solace there, as I have found.

"WHERE LIES THE LAND?"

Where lies the Land to which yon Ship must go?
Fresh as a lark mounting at break of day,
Festively she puts forth in trim array;
Is she for tropic suns, or polar snow?
What boots the inquiry?—Neither friend nor foe
She cares for; let her travel where she may,   20
She finds familiar names, a beaten way
Ever before her, and a wind to blow.
Yet still I ask, what haven is her mark?
And, almost as it was when ships were rare,
(From time to time, like Pilgrims, here and there
Crossing the waters) doubt, and something dark,
Of the old Sea some reverential fear,
Is with me at thy farewell, joyous Bark!

TO SLEEP

A FLOCK of sheep that leisurely pass by,
One after one; the sound of rain, and bees
Murmuring; the fall of rivers, winds and seas,
Smooth fields, white sheets of water, and pure sky;
I have thought of all by turns, and yet do lie
Sleepless! and soon the small birds' melodies
Must hear, first uttered from my orchard trees;
And the first cuckoo's melancholy cry.
Even thus last night, and two nights more, I lay
10   And could not win thee, Sleep! by any stealth:
So do not let me wear to-night away:
Without Thee what is all the morning's wealth?
Come, blessed barrier between day and day,
Dear mother of fresh thoughts and joyous health!

MUTABILITY

FROM low to high doth dissolution climb,
And sink from high to low, along a scale
Of awful notes, whose concord shall not fail;
A musical but melancholy chime,
Which they can hear who meddle not with crime,
20   Nor avarice, nor over-anxious care.
Truth fails not; but her outward forms that bear
The longest date do melt like frosty rime,
That in the morning whitened hill and plain
And is no more; drop like the tower sublime
Of yesterday, which royally did wear
His crown of weeds, but could not even sustain
Some casual shout that broke the silent air,
Or the unimaginable touch of Time.

22 **rime** An icy deposit resembling frost but formed from fog **or** moisture-laden air

INSIDE THE KING'S COLLEGE CHAPEL, CAMBRIDGE

TAX not the royal Saint with vain expense,
With ill-matched aims the Architect who planned—
Albeit labouring for a scanty band
Of white robed Scholars only—this immense
And glorious Work of fine intelligence!
Give all thou canst; high Heaven rejects the lore
Of nicely-calculated less or more;
So deemed the man who fashioned for the sense
These lofty pillars, spread that branching roof
Self-poised, and scooped into ten thousand cells,   10
Where light and shade repose, where music dwells
Lingering—and wandering on as loth to die;
Like thoughts whose very sweetness yieldeth proof
That they were born for immortality.

"SCORN NOT THE SONNET"

SCORN not the Sonnet; Critic, you have frowned,
Mindless of its just honours; with this key
Shakspeare unlocked his heart; the melody
Of this small lute gave ease to Petrarch's wound;
A thousand times this pipe did Tasso sound;
With it Camöens soothed an exile's grief;   21
The Sonnet glittered a gay myrtle leaf
Amid the cypress with which Dante crowned
His visionary brow: a glow-worm lamp,
It cheered mild Spenser, called from Faery-land
To struggle through dark ways; and when a damp
Fell round the path of Milton, in his hand
The Thing became a trumpet; whence he blew
Soul-animating strains—alas, too few!

1 **royal Saint** Henry VI (1421-1471), the founder of King's College 18 **Petrarch** (1304-1374) was an Italian writer of sonnets 19 **Tasso** (1544-1595) was an Italian poet 20 **Camöens** (1524-1580) was a one-eyed Portuguese epic and lyric poet who was banished from Lisbon and shipwrecked off the coast of Cochin China 22 **Dante** (1265-1321) was the greatest of Italian poets

"he Was a Phantom of Delight"

SHE was a Phantom of delight
When first she gleamed upon my sight;
A lovely Apparition, sent
To be a moment's ornament;
Her eyes as stars of Twilight fair;
Like Twilight's, too, her dusky hair;
But all things else about her drawn
From May-time and the cheerful Dawn;
A dancing Shape, an Image gay,
To haunt, to startle, and way-lay.

I saw her upon nearer view,
A Spirit, yet a Woman too!
Her household motions light and free,
And steps of virgin-liberty;
A countenance in which did meet
Sweet records, promises as sweet;
A Creature not too bright or good
For human nature's daily food;
For transient sorrows, simple wiles,
Praise, blame, love, kisses, tears, and smiles.

And now I see with eye serene
The very pulse of the machine;
A Being breathing thoughtful breath,
A Traveller between life and death;
The reason firm, the temperate will,
Endurance, foresight, strength, and skill;
A perfect Woman, nobly planned,
To warn, to comfort, and command;
And yet a Spirit still, and bright
With something of angelic light.

"I Wandered Lonely as a Cloud"

I WANDERED lonely as a cloud
That floats on high o'er vales and hills,
When all at once I saw a crowd,
A host, of golden daffodils;
Beside the lake, beneath the trees,
Fluttering and dancing in the breeze.

Continuous as the stars that shine
And twinkle on the milky way,
They stretched in never-ending line
Along the margin of a bay: 10
Ten thousand saw I at a glance,
Tossing their heads in sprightly dance.

The waves beside them danced; but they
Out-did the sparkling waves in glee:
A poet could not but be gay,
In such a jocund company:
I gazed—and gazed—but little thought
What wealth the show to me had brought:

For oft, when on my couch I lie
In vacant or in pensive mood,   20
They flash upon that inward eye
Which is the bliss of solitude;
And then my heart with pleasure fills,
And dances with the daffodils.

Ode to Duty

"Jam non consilio bonus, sed more eò perductus, ut non tantum
rectè facere possim, sed nisi rectè facere non possim."

STERN Daughter of the Voice of God!
O Duty! if that name thou love
Who are a light to guide, a rod
To check the erring, and reprove;
Thou, who art victory and law
When empty terrors overawe;
From vain temptations dost set free;
And calm'st the weary strife of frail humanity!

There are who ask not if thine eye
10   Be on them; who, in love and truth,
Where no misgiving is, rely
Upon the genial sense of youth:
Glad Hearts! without reproach or blot;
Who do thy work, and know it not:
Oh! if through confidence misplaced
They fail, thy saving arms, dread Power! around them cast.

Serene will be our days and bright,
And happy will our nature be,
When love is an unerring light,
20   And joy its own security.
And they a blissful course may hold
Even now, who, not unwisely bold,
Live in the spirit of this creed;
Yet seek thy firm support, according to their need.

I, loving freedom, and untried;
No sport of every random gust,
Yet being to myself a guide,

Title: This Latin motto ("Guided not so much by counsel or de-
sign as by habit or custom, I am not only capable of doing good,
I am incapable of doing evil") Wordsworth derived from Seneca,
Moral Epistles, CXX, 10. The motto first appeared with the poem
in the edition of 1837

Too blindly have reposed my trust:
And oft, when in my heart was heard
Thy timely mandate, I deferred   30
The task, in smoother walks to stray;
But thee I now would serve more strictly, if I may.

Through no disturbance of my soul,
Or strong compunction in me wrought,
I supplicate for thy control;
But in the quietness of thought:
Me this unchartered freedom tires;
I feel the weight of chance-desires:
My hopes no more must change their name,
I long for a repose that ever is the same.   40

Stern Lawgiver! yet thou dost wear
The Godhead's most benignant grace;
Nor know we anything so fair
As is the smile upon thy face:
Flowers laugh before thee on their beds
And fragrance in thy footing treads;
Thou dost preserve the stars from wrong;
And the most ancient heavens, through Thee, are fresh and
    strong.

To humbler functions, awful Power!
I call thee: I myself commend   50
Unto thy guidance from this hour;
Oh, let my weakness have an end!
Give unto me, made lowly wise,
The spirit of self-sacrifice;
The confidence of reason give;
And in the light of truth thy Bondman let me live!

The Solitary Reaper

BEHOLD her, single in the field,
Yon solitary Highland Lass!
Reaping and singing by herself;
Stop here, or gently pass!

Alone she cuts and binds the grain,
And sings a melancholy strain;
O listen! for the Vale profound
Is overflowing with the sound.

No Nightingale did ever chaunt
10   More welcome notes to weary bands
Of travellers in some shady haunt,
Among Arabian sands:
A voice so thrilling ne'er was heard
In spring-time from the Cuckoo-bird,
Breaking the silence of the seas
Among the farthest Hebrides.

Will no one tell me what she sings?—
Perhaps the plaintive numbers flow
For old, unhappy, far-off things,
20   And battles long ago:
Or is it some more humble lay,
Familiar matter of to-day?
Some natural sorrow, loss, or pain,
That has been, and may be again?

Whate'er the theme, the Maiden sang
As if her song could have no ending;
I saw her singing at her work,
And o'er the sickle bending:—
I listened, motionless and still;
30   And, as I mounted up the hill,
The music in my heart I bore,
Long after it was heard no more.

"My Heart Leaps Up"

My heart leaps up when I behold
    A rainbow in the sky:
So was it when my life began;
So is it now I am a man;

16 **Hebrides** A group of islands off the northwest coast of Scotland

So be it when I shall grow old,
    Or let me die!
The Child is father of the Man;
And I could wish my days to be
Bound each to each by natural piety.

Ode

INTIMATIONS OF IMMORTALITY FROM
RECOLLECTIONS OF EARLY CHILDHOOD

I

THERE was a time when meadow, grove, and stream,
The earth, and every common sight,
    To me did seem
    Apparelled in celestial light,
The glory and the freshness of a dream.
It is not now as it hath been of yore;—
    Turn whereso'er I may,
      By night or day,
The things which I have seen I now can see no more.

II

    The Rainbow comes and goes,   10
    And lovely is the Rose,
    The Moon doth with delight
Look round her when the heavens are bare,
    Waters on a starry night
    Are beautiful and fair;
  The sunshine is a glorious birth;
  But yet I know, where'er I go,
That there hath past away a glory from the earth.

III

Now, while the birds thus sing a joyous song,
  And while the young lambs bound   20
    As to the tabor's sound,

21 **tabor** A small drum ordinarily used to accompany a pipe or trumpet

To me alone there came a thought of grief:
A timely utterance gave that thought relief,
      And I again am strong:
The cataracts blow their trumpets from the steep;
No more shall grief of mine the season wrong;
I hear the Echoes through the mountains throng,
The Winds come to me from the fields of sleep,
      And all the earth is gay;
30   Land and sea
    Give themselves up to jollity,
      And with the heart of May
    Doth every Beast keep holiday;—
      Thou Child of Joy,
Shout round me, let me hear thy shouts, thou happy
    Shepherd-boy!

IV

Ye blessèd Creatures, I have heard the call
    Ye to each other make; I see
The heavens laugh with you in your jubilee;
40   My heart is at your festival,
      My head hath its coronal,
The fulness of your bliss, I feel—I feel it all.
      O evil day! if I were sullen
      While Earth herself is adorning,
        This sweet May-morning,
      And the Children are culling
        On every side,
      In a thousand valleys far and wide,
      Fresh flowers; while the sun shines warm,
50 And the Babe leaps up on his Mother's arm:—
      I hear, I hear, with joy I hear!
      —But there's a Tree, of many, one,
A single Field which I have looked upon,
Both of them speak of something that is gone:
      The Pansy at my feet
      Doth the same tale repeat:
Whither is fled the visionary gleam?
Where is it now, the glory and the dream?

V

Our birth is but a sleep and a forgetting:
The Soul that rises with us, our life's Star,   **60**
      Hath had elsewhere its setting,
        And cometh from afar:
      Not in entire forgetfulness,
      And not in utter nakedness,
But trailing clouds of glory do we come
      From God, who is our home:
Heaven lies about us in our infancy!
Shades of the prison-house begin to close
      Upon the growing Boy,
But He beholds the light, and whence it flows,   **70**
      He sees it in his joy;
The Youth, who daily farther from the east
      Must travel, still is Nature's Priest,
      And by the vision splendid
      Is on his way attended;
At length the Man perceives it die away,
And fade into the light of common day.

VI

Earth fills her lap with pleasures of her own;
Yearnings she hath in her own natural kind,
And, even with something of a Mother's mind,   **80**
      And no unworthy aim,
      The homely Nurse doth all she can
To make her Foster-child, her Inmate Man,
      Forget the glories he hath known,
And that imperial palace whence he came.

VII

Behold the Child among his new-born blisses,
A six years' Darling of a pigmy size!
See, where 'mid work of his own hand he lies,
Fretted by sallies of his mother's kisses,
With light upon him from his father's eyes!   **90**
See, at his feet, some little plan or chart,
Some fragment from his dream of human life,
Shaped by himself with newly-learned art;
      A wedding or a festival,

A mourning or a funeral;
    And this hath now his heart,
    And unto this he frames his song:
    Then will he fit his tongue
To dialogues of business, love, or strife;
100   But it will not be long
    Ere this be thrown aside,
    And with new joy and pride
The little Actor cons another part;
Filling from time to time his "humorous stage"
With all the Persons, down to palsied Age,
That Life brings with her in her equipage;
        As if his whole vocation
        Were endless imitation.

VIII

Thou, whose exterior semblance doth belie
110   Thy Soul's immensity;
Thou best Philosopher, who yet dost keep
Thy heritage, thou Eye among the blind,
That, deaf and silent, read'st the eternal deep,
Haunted for ever by the eternal mind,—
        Mighty Prophet! Seer blest!
        On whom those truths do rest,
Which we are toiling all our lives to find,
In darkness lost, the darkness of the grave;
Thou, over whom thy Immortality
120 Broods like the Day, a Master o'er a Slave,
A Presence which is not to be put by;
Thou little Child, yet glorious in the might
Of heaven-born freedom on thy being's height,
Why with such earnest pains dost thou provoke
The years to bring the inevitable yoke,
Thus blindly with thy blessedness at strife?
Full soon thy Soul shall have her earthly freight,
And custom lie upon thee with a weight,
Heavy as frost, and deep almost as life!

104 Quoted from the dedicatory sonnet to Samuel Daniel's
Musophilus (1599)

IX

O joy! that in our embers   130
Is something that doth live,
That nature yet remembers
What was so fugitive!
The thought of our past years in me doth breed
Perpetual benediction: not indeed
For that which is most worthy to be blest;
Delight and liberty, the simple creed
Of Childhood, whether busy or at rest,
With new-fledged hope still fluttering in his breast:—
    Not for these I raise   140
    The song of thanks and praise;
  But for those obstinate questionings
  Of sense and outward things,
  Fallings from us, vanishings;
  Blank misgivings of a Creature
Moving about in worlds not realised,
High instincts before which our mortal Nature
Did tremble like a guilty Thing surprised:
    But for those first affections,
    Those shadowy recollections,   150
  Which, be they what they may,
Are yet the fountain-light of all our day,
Are yet a master-light of all our seeing;
  Uphold us, cherish, and have power to make
Our noisy years seem moments in the being
Of the eternal Silence: truths that wake,
    To perish never:
Which neither listlessness, nor mad endeavour,
    Nor Man nor Boy,
Nor all that is at enmity with joy,   160
Can utterly abolish or destroy!
  Hence in a season of calm weather
    Though inland far we be,
Our Souls have sight of that immortal sea
    Which brought us hither,
  Can in a moment travel thither,
And see the Children sport upon the shore,
And hear the mighty waters rolling evermore.

X

Then sing, ye Birds, sing, sing a joyous song!
170   And let the young Lambs bound
      As to the tabor's sound!
We in thought will join your throng,
      Ye that pipe and ye that play,
      Ye that through your hearts today
      Feel the gladness of the May!
What though the radiance which was once so bright
Be now for ever taken from my sight,
      Though nothing can bring back the hour
Of splendour in the grass, of glory in the flower;
180   We will grieve not, rather find
      Strength in what remains behind;
      In the primal sympathy
      Which having been must ever be;
      In the soothing thoughts that spring
      Out of human suffering;
      In the faith that looks through death,
In years that bring the philosophic mind.

XI

And O, ye Fountains, Meadows, Hills, and Groves,
Forebode not any severing of our loves!
190 Yet in my heart of hearts I feel your might;
I only have relinquished one delight
To live beneath your more habitual sway.
I love the Brooks which down their channels fret,
Even more than when I tripped lightly as they;
The innocent brightness of a new-born Day
      Is lovely yet;
The Clouds that gather round the setting sun
Do take a sober colouring from an eye
That hath kept watch o'er man's mortality;
200 Another race hath been, and other palms are won.
Thanks to the human heart by which we live,
Thanks to its tenderness, its joys, and fears,
To me the meanest flower that blows can give
Thoughts that do often lie too deep for tears.

Elegiac Stanzas

SUGGESTED BY A PICTURE OF PEELE CASTLE, IN A STORM,
PAINTED BY SIR GEORGE BEAUMONT

I WAS thy neighbour once, thou rugged Pile!
Four summer weeks I dwelt in sight of thee:
I saw thee every day; and all the while
Thy Form was sleeping on a glassy sea.

So pure the sky, so quiet was the air!
So like, so very like, was day to day!
Whene'er I looked, thy Image still was there;
It trembled, but it never passed away.

How perfect was the calm! it seemed no sleep;
No mood, which season takes away, or brings: 10
I could have fancied that the mighty Deep
Was even the gentlest of all gentle Things.

Ah! then, if mine had been the Painter's hand,
To express what then I saw; and add the gleam,
The light that never was, on sea or land,
The consecration, and the Poet's dream;

I would have planted thee, thou hoary Pile
Amid a world how different from this!
Beside a sea that could not cease to smile;
On tranquil land, beneath a sky of bliss.   20

Thou shouldst have seemed a treasure-house divine
Of peaceful years; a chronicle of heaven;—
Of all the sunbeams that did ever shine
The very sweetest had to thee been given.

A Picture had it been of lasting ease,
Elysian quiet, without toil or strife;
No motion but the moving tide, a breeze,
Or merely silent Nature's breathing life.

Such, in the fond illusion of my heart,
80 Such Picture would I at that time have made:
And seen the soul of truth in every part,
A steadfast peace that might not be betrayed.

So once it would have been,—'tis so no more;
I have submitted to a new control:
A power is gone, which nothing can restore;
A deep distress hath humanised my Soul.

Not for a moment could I now behold
A smiling sea, and be what I have been:
The feeling of my loss will ne'er be old;
40 This, which I know, I speak with mind serene.

Then, Beaumont, Friend! who would have been the Friend,
If he had lived, of Him whom I deplore,
This work of thine I blame not, but commend;
This sea in anger, and that dismal shore.

O 'tis a passionate Work!—yet wise and well,
Well chosen is the spirit that is here;
That Hulk which labours in the deadly swell,
This rueful sky, this pageantry of fear!

And this huge Castle, standing here sublime,
50 I love to see the look with which it braves,
Cased in the unfeeling armour of old time,
The lightning, the fierce wind, and trampling waves.

Farewell, farewell the heart that lives alone,
Housed in a dream, at distance from the Kind!
Such happiness, wherever it be known,
Is to be pitied; for 'tis surely blind.

But welcome fortitude, and patient cheer,
And frequent sights of what is to be borne!
Such sights, or worse, as are before me here.—
60 Not without hope we suffer and we mourn.

42 **Him** Wordsworth's brother, Captain John Wordsworth, who
went down with his ship, the *Earl of Abergavenny*, off the Bill
of Portland, near Weymouth, the night of 5 February 1805

Character of the Happy Warrior

Who is the happy Warrior? Who is he
That every man in arms should wish to be?
—It is the generous Spirit, who, when brought
Among the tasks of real life, hath wrought
Upon the plan that pleased his boyish thought:
Whose high endeavours are an inward light
That makes the path before him always bright:
Who, with a natural instinct to discern
What knowledge can perform, is diligent to learn;
Abides by this resolve, and stops not there,   10
But makes his moral being his prime care;
Who, doomed to go in company with Pain,
And Fear, and Bloodshed, miserable train!
Turns his necessity to glorious gain;
In face of these doth exercise a power
Which is our human nature's highest dower;
Controls them and subdues, transmutes, bereaves
Of their bad influence, and their good receives:
By objects, which might force the soul to abate
Her feeling, rendered more compassionate;   20
Is placable—because occasions rise
So often that demand such sacrifice;
More skilful in self-knowledge, even more pure,
As tempted more; more able to endure,
As more exposed to suffering and distress;
Thence, also, more alive to tenderness.
—'Tis he whose law is reason; who depends
Upon that law as on the best of friends;
Whence, in a state where men are tempted still
To evil for a guard against worse ill,   30
And what in quality or act is best
Doth seldom on a right foundation rest,
He labours good on good to fix, and owes
To virtue every triumph that he knows:
—Who, if he rise to station of command,
Rises by open means; and there will stand
On honourable terms, or else retire,
And in himself possess his own desire;

Who comprehends his trust, and to the same
40   Keeps faithful with a singleness of aim;
And therefore does not stoop, nor lie in wait
For wealth, or honours, or for worldly state;
Whom they must follow; on whose head must fall,
Like showers of manna, if they come at all:
Whose powers shed round him in the common strife,
Or mild concerns of ordinary life,
A constant influence, a peculiar grace;
But who, if he be called upon to face
Some awful moment to which Heaven has joined
50   Great issues, good or bad for human kind,
Is happy as a Lover; and attired
With sudden brightness, like a Man inspired;
And, through the heat of conflict, keeps the law
In calmness made, and sees what he foresaw;
Or if an unexpected call succeed,
Come when it will, is equal to the need:
—He who, though thus endued as with a sense
And faculty for storm and turbulence,
Is yet a Soul whose master-bias leans
60   To homefelt pleasures and to gentle scenes;
Sweet images! which, wheresoe'er he be,
Are at his heart; and such fidelity
It is his darling passion to approve;
More brave for this, that he hath much to love:—
'Tis, finally, the Man, who, lifted high,
Conspicuous object in a Nation's eye,
Or left unthought-of in obscurity,—
Who, with a toward or untoward lot,
Prosperous or adverse, to his wish or not—
70   Plays, in the many games of life, that one
Where what he most doth value must be won:
Whom neither shape of danger can dismay,
Nor thought of tender happiness betray;
Who, not content that former worth stand fast,
Looks forward, persevering to the last,
From well to better, daily self-surpast:
Who, whether praise of him must walk the earth
For ever, and to noble deeds give birth,
Or he must fall, to sleep without his fame,
80   And leave a dead unprofitable name—

Finds comfort in himself and in his cause;
And, while the mortal mist is gathering, draws
His breath in confidence of Heaven's applause:
This is the happy Warrior; this is He
That every Man in arms should wish to be.

LINES

COMPOSED AT GRASMERE, DURING A WALK ONE EVENING,
AFTER A STORMY DAY, THE AUTHOR HAVING JUST READ
IN A NEWSPAPER THAT THE DISSOLUTION OF MR. FOX
WAS HOURLY EXPECTED.

1806. 1807

Loud is the Vale! the Voice is up
With which she speaks when storms are gone,
A mighty unison of streams!
Of all her Voice, One!

Loud is the Vale;—this inland Depth
In peace is roaring like the Sea;
Yon star upon the mountain-top
Is listening quietly.

Sad was I, even to pain deprest,
Importunate and heavy load!   10
The Comforter hath found me here,
Upon this lonely road;

And many thousands now are sad—
Wait the fulfilment of their fear;
For he must die who is their stay,
Their glory disappear.

A Power is passing from the earth
To breathless Nature's dark abyss;
But when the great and good depart
What is it more than this—   20

That Man, who is from God sent forth,
Doth yet again to God return?—
Such ebb and flow must ever be,
Then wherefore should we mourn?

BIBLIOGRAPHY

EDITIONS

The Poetical Works of William Wordsworth, 5 vols., edited by Ernest de Selincourt and Helen Darbishire. London, 1940-1949.
The Complete Poetical Works of William Wordsworth (Cambridge edition), edited by A. J. George. Boston, 1904.
The Poetical Works of William Wordsworth, 8 vols., edited by William Knight. London, 1896.

BIOGRAPHIES

Harper, George McLean, *William Wordsworth, His Life, Works, and Influence.* New York, 1929.
Legouis, Émile, *The Early Life of William Wordsworth, 1770-1798,* translated by J. W. Matthews. New York, 1918.
Meyer, George Wilbur. *Wordsworth's Formative Years,* University of Michigan Publications, Language and Literature, Vol. XX. Ann Arbor, 1943.
Moorman, Mary, *William Wordsworth, A Biography: The Early Years, 1770-1803.* New York, 1957.

CRITICISM

Arnold, Matthew, Preface to *Poems of Wordsworth.* London, 1879.
Bradley, A. C., "Wordsworth," *Oxford Lectures in Poetry.* London, 1904.
Campbell, Oscar James, and Mueschke, Paul, "Wordsworth's Aesthetic Development, 1795-1802," *Essays and Studies in English and Comparative Literature,* University of Michigan Publications, Language and Literature, Vol. X. Ann Arbor, 1933.

115